Guitar: The First 100 Jazz Chords for Guitar

How to Learn and Play Jazz Guitar Chords for Beginners

Guitar: The First 100 Jazz Chords for Guitar

How to Learn and Play Jazz Guitar Chords for Beginners

ISBN: 978-1-911267-62-1

Published by **www.fundamental-changes.com**

www.fundamental-changes.com

Twitter: **@guitar_joseph**
Over 8500 fans on Facebook: **FundamentalChangesInGuitar**
Instagram: **FundamentalChanges**

**For over 250 Free Guitar Lessons with Videos Check Out
www.fundamental-changes.com**

Cover Image Copyright: Shutterstock: Robin Fritzson / Bahadir Yeniceri

Contents

Introduction

Jazz chords are sometimes spoken of in hushed tones by musicians, and this is particularly true of guitarists. There seems to be an aura of mystique around these chords and they often have rather complex names and crunchy sounds.

However, as much as the institutions (who charge lots of money to take a three-year degree course) would have you believe jazz chords are complex and inaccessible, this book sets out to dispel the myths around playing jazz chords and make them available to mere mortals like you and me.

I have written three other books on jazz guitar chords.

Guitar Chords in Context

Jazz Guitar Chord Mastery

And

Voice Leading Jazz Guitar.

All these books, in my humble opinion, do a great job of getting deep into the theory and application of jazz chords and provide a detailed framework for anyone wishing to build a comprehensive understanding and musical appreciation of jazz.

If you're starting out, or maybe if you've bought another of my books, **The First 100 Chords for Guitar**, I would highly recommend that you check out **Guitar Chords in Context** if you want to learn everything you'll ever need about music theory and, more importantly, it's application.

Every book I write is heavy on application. "Theory" is useless if you don't know how it *sounds* or understand how and when to apply it. On your first day at school, you weren't given a dictionary and then sent off to speak English fluently. You learnt to use language correctly (and in context) through practice and application.

Guitar Chords in Context isn't even *that* jazzy… it teaches you everything you need to know about chords for Rock, Pop, Blues and Jazz. It's a complete course in modern guitar harmony for rockers!

So then, if I've written three books on jazz chords already, why am I sitting here writing another one?

Well, not every student wants a totally comprehensive course. It might just be that you want to put your toe in the waters of jazz to make your chord playing a bit more interesting. Maybe you just want to try on a few of those rich-sounding chords for size and see what fits.

Many students who come to me looking to learn jazz simply want to find some new sounds to complement their song writing, or help them to create new moods in music.

You can think of this book as **Jazz Guitar Chord Mastery** "Lite". The idea is to give you everything you need as effectively as possible and go easy on the theory except for providing you with the ideas that are relevant for putting all these chords together into some sort of music.

As always, there will be tons of musical examples and ideas for you to get your teeth into, and when you finish working through them you will be a better, more versatile guitarist. However, the emphasis throughout is on teaching you the most essential chords that take care of 80% of commonly played jazz chords on guitar.

Disclaimer: Throughout this book I will be borrowing from the three jazz chord books listed above. If you own any one of them you will notice many similarities.

If you already own any of those titles, this book isn't aimed at you! This book takes some of the more basic concepts from each book and combines them to make a comprehensive primer for the student who is new to jazz guitar. By using ideas, and more importantly diagrams and notation from the above three books, I provide you with a great book that gives a great overview of using jazz chords.

Once you have worked through this book you will find any of the above publications very helpful if you want to get *really* deep into many concepts that aren't touched on here.

Right, let's get started with some simple theory that will give context to everything that comes after.

Get the Audio

The audio files for this book are available to download for free from **www.fundamental-changes.com**, and the link is in the top right corner. Simply select this book title from the drop-down menu and follow the instructions to get the audio.

We recommend that you download the files directly to your computer, not to your tablet, and extract them there before adding them to your media library. You can then put them on your tablet, iPod or burn them to CD. On the download page, there is a help PDF, and we also provide technical support via the contact form.

Kindle / eReaders

To get the most out of this book, remember that you can double tap any image to enlarge it. Turn off 'column viewing' and hold your Kindle in landscape mode.

For over 250 Free Guitar Lessons with Videos Check out:
www.fundamental-changes.com

Twitter: @guitar_joseph
FB: FundamentalChangesInGuitar
Instagram: FundamentalChanges

Chapter One: Four Different Families of Chords

We need to start somewhere, so I'm going to assume you can play basic open chords, barre chords and the C Major scale.

If you struggle with any of the above you may find the following information a little challenging. If this is the case, I strongly recommend that you check out **The First 100 Chords for Guitar** before launching into this book.

Forming chords.

A chord is defined as any group of three or more notes played together. They are normally formed by stacking notes on top of each other from a particular scale. Most of the chords in this book are formed from *harmonising* the major scale.

To form a chord, we simply stack alternate notes from a scale. For example, in the scale of C Major:

C D E F G A B C

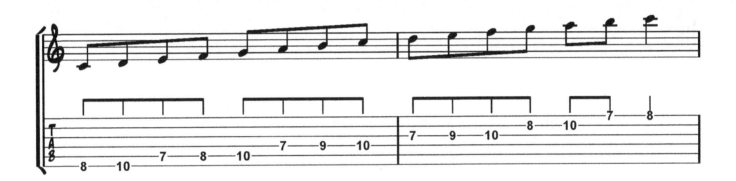

We take the first, third and fifth notes (C E and G), and play them together to form a C Major chord.

(C) D (E) F (G) A B C

Example 1a:

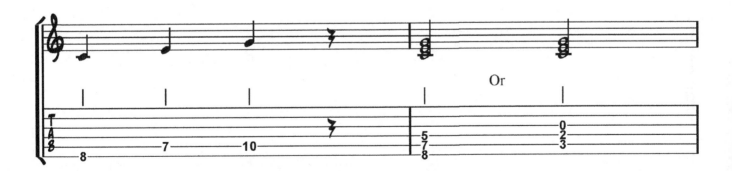

If you notice, we took the *first* note C, then skipped the next note (D) and landed on the *third* note E. We repeated this process and skipped the fourth note (F) and landed on the *fifth* note G. The notes played together in this way are called a *triad*.

The first, third and fifth notes of a major scale form a major chord. This is true of any major scale. This chord is given the formula 1 3 5.

The formula 1 3 5 in C Major gives us the notes C E and G, however, we can alter any of the notes to form a different type of chord. For example, if we *flatten* the third we generate the formula 1 b3 5. We now have the notes C *Eb* G.

Example 1b:

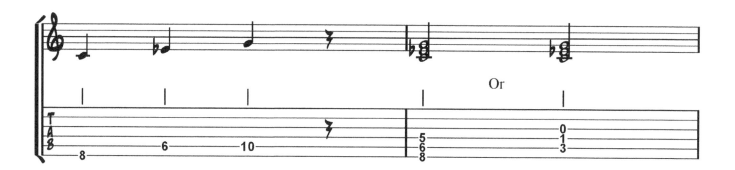

As you can hear, this structure has a very different sound from the previous major chord.

Any chord with the structure 1 b3 5 is a minor chord. In fact, *any* chord that contains a b3 is defined as a minor sound.

We can also flatten the 5th of the chord. The structure 1 3 b5 is not very common in music although it does sometimes occur in jazz. However, the structure 1 b3 b5 occurs frequently. It is called a *diminished* or occasionally a *minor b5* chord.

The formula 1 b3 b5 built on a root of C generates the notes C Eb Gb.

Example 1c:

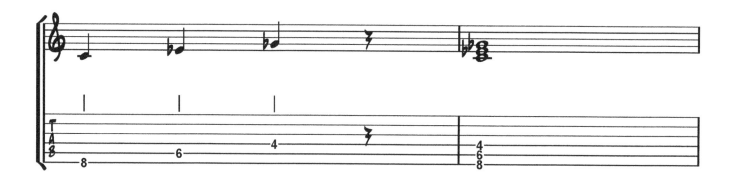

The above shape is a bit of a stretch to play on the guitar, but the notes do not have to be played in this order. They can be played more comfortably like this:

Example 1d:

To achieve this voicing, I moved the b3 of the chord up by one octave.

As you can hear, the diminished chord has a dark and sinister air to it.

The three triads you have learned so far are

1 3 5 Major

1 b3 5 Minor

1 b3 b5 Diminished or just 'Dim'

Most chords you come across in music, no matter how complicated can normally be categorised into one of these basic types. Jazz chord progressions are normally formed from richer sounding '7th' chords, which are the focus of this book.

There is, however, one more permutation that crops up occasionally, it is the augmented triad, 1 3 #5.

From a root note of C, the notes generated by this formula are C E G#. There are two tones between each of the notes of the chord.

Example 1e:

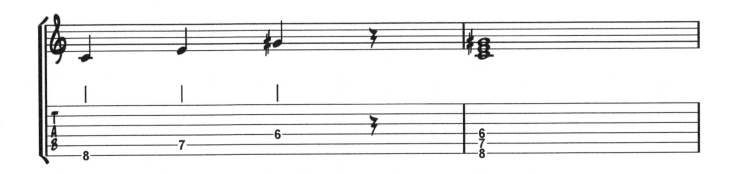

Two useful voicings of the augmented (Aug) triad are

Example 1f:

Finally, there are two types of triad that do *not* include a 3rd. These chords are normally named 'suspended' (or just 'sus' chords), as the lack of the 3rd gives an unresolved feel to their character.

In a 'sus' 2 chord the 3rd is replaced with the 2nd of the scale, and in a sus4 chord, the 3rd is replaced with the 4th of the scale.

In C, the notes generated by the formula 1 2 5 are C D and G.

Example 1g

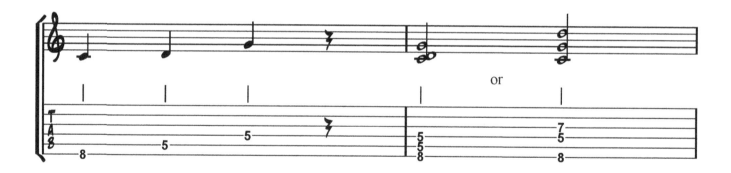

The notes generated by the formula 1 4 5 are C F and G.

Example 1h

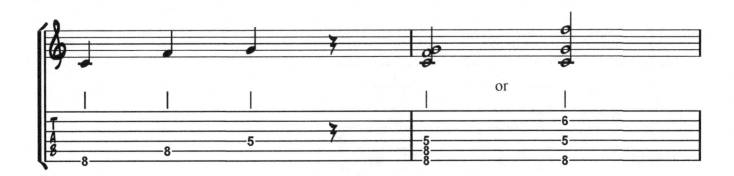

It is first important that you learn to play some useful chord voicings of these basic triads as they do sometimes occur in jazz chord charts, especially in early 'swing' jazz.

In any chord, it is acceptable to *double* any note. For example, a major chord could contain two roots, two 5ths and only one 3rd. There were rules to govern their use in 'classical' times, although these days there are common chord shapes or 'grips' on the guitar that are frequently used.

As the focus of this book is on 7th chords, which are more common in jazz, only a few of the basic triad chord shapes are shown here.

Major Chord Shapes:

Example 1i:

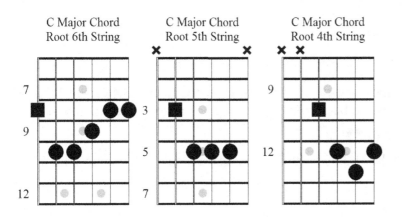

Minor Chord Shapes:

Example 1j:

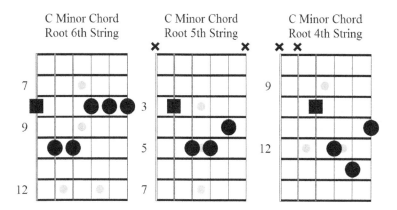

Diminished (minor b5) Chord Shapes:

Example 1k:

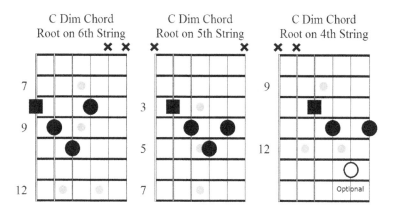

You probably already know most of these shapes, but if you don't, my advice is to ignore them for now while we get focused on 7th chords. You can come back to these voicings as a reference when you need them.

To create a major 7th chord we simply extend the '1 3 5' formula by an extra note so it becomes '1 3 5 7'.

Instead of C E G we now have C E G B:

(C) D (E) F (G) A (B)

Don't worry about learning the following few chord shapes. The following shapes are just for illustration, some of them aren't great voicings and we and we will look at more useful voicings in chapter 2. For now, just try to get the sound of the chords into your head..

Example 1l:

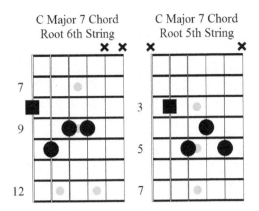

C Major 7 Chord
Root 6th String

C Major 7 Chord
Root 5th String

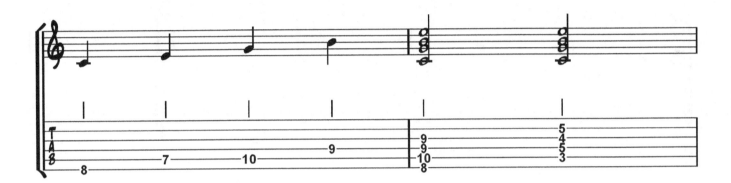

In these voicings, I have changed the order of the notes to make the chord playable on the guitar. The chord is now voiced 1 5 7 3.

As the major 7th's chord formula is 1 3 5 7, you might expect that the minor 7th's formula would be 1 b3 5 7. This, however, is *not* the case.

To create a minor 7 chord we add a *b7* to a minor triad. The formula is 1 b3 5 *b7*.

The formula 1 b3 5 b7 built on a root note of C generates the notes C Eb G Bb.

Example 1m:

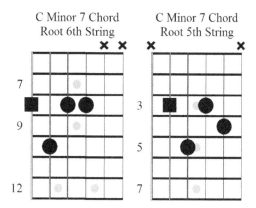

C Minor 7 Chord
Root 6th String

C Minor 7 Chord
Root 5th String

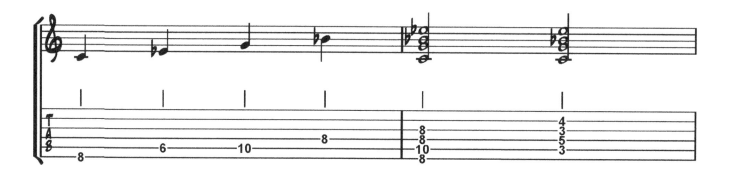

Once again, the notes in the lower chord voicing have been rearranged to make the voicing playable on the guitar.

As you're probably wondering, a minor triad with a *natural 7* on the top 1 b3 5 **7** is called a *"minor major 7th"* or m(Maj7) chord. They are given this name because they are minor triads with a *major* 7th added on top.

When we extend a minor b5 chord to become a 7th chord, we once again add a *b7*, not a natural 7. In fact, it is a general rule that if a triad has a b3, it is more common to add a b7 to form a four-note '7th' chord.

As you can see in the previous paragraph, this is not always the case, so be careful when applying that 'rule'.

A (diminished) minor b5 chord with an added b7 has the formula 1 b3 b5 b7 and generates the notes C Eb Gb Bb when built from the root note of C. This chord is named 'Minor 7 flat 5' or m7b5 for short. It also is common for m7b5 chords to be referred to as 'half diminished' chords.

Example 1n:

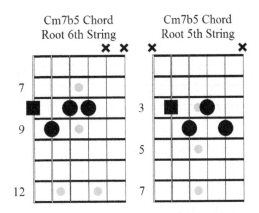

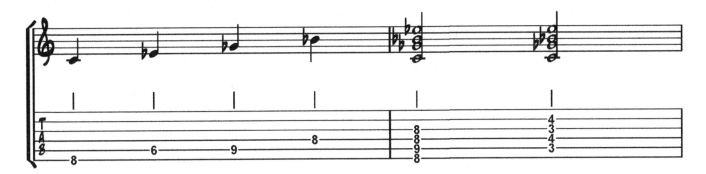

Finally, we come to one of the most common chords in jazz; the dominant 7 chord. It is formed by adding a b7 to a major triad. 1 3 5 b7. With a root of C this formula generates the notes C E G Bb.

Because of the fundamental major triad 1 3 5, this chord is a 'major' type chord, but the added b7 gives it an extra bit of tension.

Example 1o:

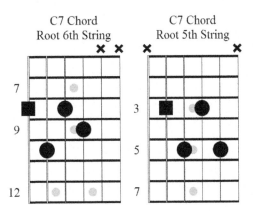

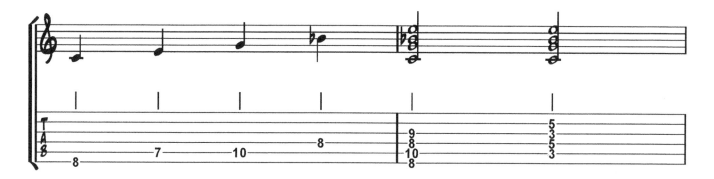

These four chord types can be summarised:

Chord Type	Formula	Short Name
Major 7	1 3 5 7	'maj7'
Dominant 7	1 3 5 b7	'7'
Minor 7	1 b3 5 b7	'm7'
Minor 7 b5	1 b3 b5 b7	'm7b5'

It is the modern way of thinking that *all* chord types in jazz function in one of the above contexts. What this means in simple terms is that even a complex chord, such as C7#5b9, can be viewed in its simplest form as just C7.

A C Minor 11 chord can be simplified to become a Cm7-type chord and a C major 9th chord can be reduced to a Cmaj7-type chord. This is very useful when viewing jazz tunes from a soloing perspective. There are a few exceptions to these rules, and these will be addressed individually.

This idea of chord 'types' or families is especially useful when we're just starting out, or when we're given a particularly difficult chord chart to read with little preparation time.

Chord families

Maj7-type chords

This is a gross simplification, but any chord name that contains a "Maj", "Major" or "6" can normally be seen as a type of a Major 7 chord. If you see BbMaj9 or Bb Maj6, more often than not it is OK to play a BbMaj7.

Now, if you're an experienced jazzer, you may be yelling at me, because sometimes it's *not* OK to substitute a Major 7 for a "6" chord. However, while you're starting out, it's a useful "ballpark" approach that will allow you to play through a tune. Do you really want to run into a brickwall when you know every chord in a tune apart from Bb6, or do you want to get through it with a very slight potential clash when you play a BbMaj7 instead?

Let's get you playing and we can worry about the tiny details later. I wasted many years worrying about this kind of thing, and as a result I didn't make the progress I could have. When you learn English as a child, you don't worry about every possible irregular verb, you just get corrected by adults and remember the exceptions.

How often do you hear a child say something like, "I ride-ed my bike"? We all know that the past tense of ride is rode, but if the child in question had to worry about every possible irregular verb when they were trying to communicate they'd never open their mouth. I promise you it's better to learn by doing.

Minor7 (m7)-type chords

The m7 chords are a bit more forgiving. Anytime you see a "min" (or "m") you can normally play a m7 chord. Again, there are a couple of specific exceptions, but anytime you see a Bbm, Bbm9, Bbm11 etc., you can simply play a Bbm7 chord.

The only time you can't do this is when you see a Bbm(Maj)7. That's a really specific voicing and should be played as written.

Dominant 7-type chords

Any Dominant 7, 9, 11, or 13 chord can be played as a dominant 7 chord. The only real exceptions are when you see a "7sus" chord, as the composer doesn't want you to play the 3rd. Again, don't worry about this for now, that is a rare occurrence. However, as you will learn later, jazz musicians play a lot of chords called "altered" dominant chords. These look terrifying on paper and have names like Bb7b9, Bb7#5 or even Bb7b5#9.

For now, ignore the algebra at the end and play them all as Bb7 chords.

Minor 7b5 (m7b5)-type chords

You won't see too many variations of m7b5 chords, but sometimes chords like Bbm9b5 or Bbm7b5b9 do occasionally crop up. Again, play both of these as a m7b5.

So there we have it, at the end of this first long chapter, you understand how to build almost every important guitar chord, and more importantly, simplify your thinking into just four important chord types.

If you see the chord progression:

Cm11 – F7#5#9 – BbMaj9 – Gm9

You now know you can simply play

Cm7 – F7 – BbMaj7 – Gm7.

OK, it isn't exactly what's written but it is close enough for government. You'll sound great, you'll get through the gig, and 99.9% of people won't even notice.

Chapter Two: Basic Common Chord Voicings

Now that we understand how the most common jazz chords are constructed, we can begin to learn some useful voicings. The voicings in this chapter are designed to 'get you through the tune'. They are the first jazz chord voicings that most guitarists learn, and will remain a part of your vocabulary from this point forward.

We will begin by learning three voicings of each of the fundamental chord types, maj7, 7, m7, and m7b5 and then apply them to a common jazz chord progression.

It is important at this point that you know where the notes are on your guitar fretboard as you will learn movable barre chord forms of each chord.

For example, we will learn a barre chord '7' shape and if you want to play this chord as a C7 you will need to place it so that the root note is C. If you wish to play it as an F7 you will have to move it so that the root note is F. In order to do this you should at least be familiar with the notes on the bottom three strings:

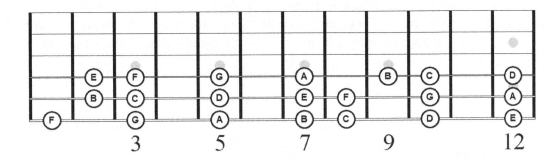

We are going to learn to play the following chord progression using three different jazz chord voicings for each chord.

Gm7b5	C7	Fm7	Dbmaj7

As you can see, this chord progression uses each of the chord types from the previous chapter once.

Let's begin by learning voicings of these chords that have their root on the 6th string. The numbers written on the notes are suggested fingerings. If you find it easier to use different fingers then please feel free to use them.

You may find it easier to play the Fm7 chord 'up an octave' at the 13th fret, this is also fine.

Example 2a:

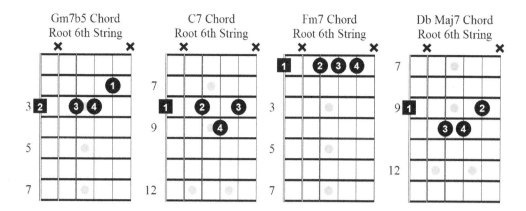

Learn these chords and then join them together so you can play example 2a. Pay attention to the 'X's that show muted strings that don't have a fretted note. You can mute them with the underside of the finger that is playing the fretted note on the lower string. For example, the open 5th string is muted by the finger playing the 6th string.

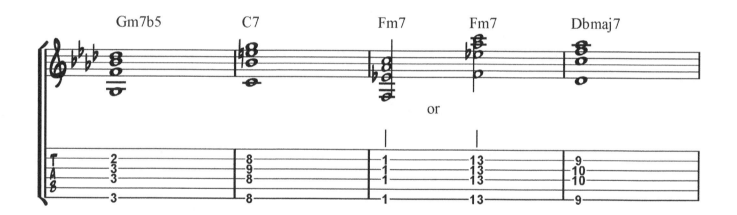

You will notice that these chord voicings move around a great deal on the fretboard. Don't worry about this for now, as when you have a few more voicings under your fingers you can start to smooth out the movements.

Next, learn the same common chords voiced with the root on the 5th string:

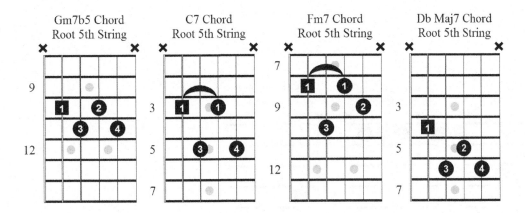

Learn the same chord sequence using just the 5th string voicings:

Example 2b:

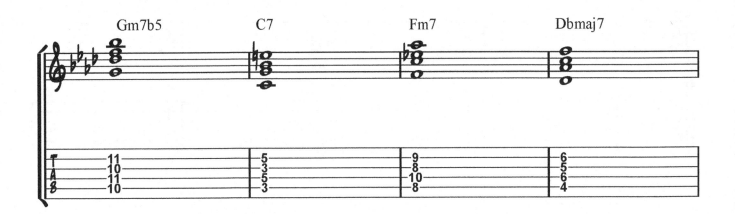

Before moving on to learning these chord types with a 4th string root, combine the 6th and 5th string chords to voice the chords closer together.

Try beginning on the 6th string for the Gm7b5 chord and then move to the closest voicing of the C7 chord on the 5th string (3rd fret) when you change. Always look for the closest possible voicing when you change chords. One way of doing this could be:

Example 2c:

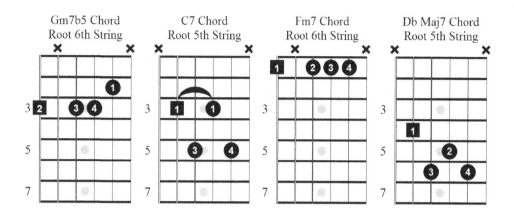

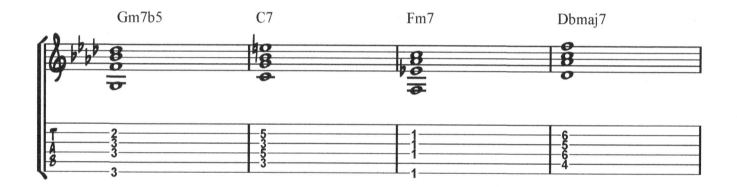

Another way to practice this is to begin on the 5th string voicing of the Gm7b5 chord and repeat the same process.

Example 2d:

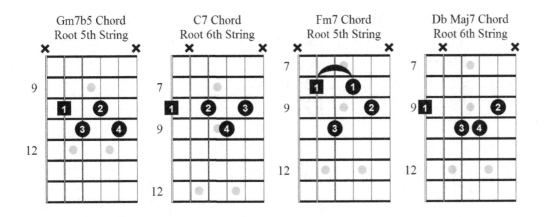

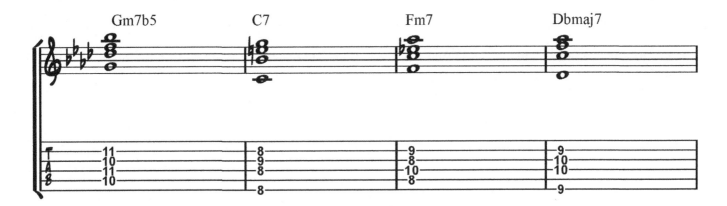

By changing strings in this way, we can always create smoother '*voice leading*' between each of the chords in the chord progression. (Voice leading is the technique of arranging chords so that each note moves the smallest possible distance during each chord change). It is also easier to play these chords at speed because the fretting hand is not moving such great distances.

Now let's look at how to play the same chords played with a 4th string root.

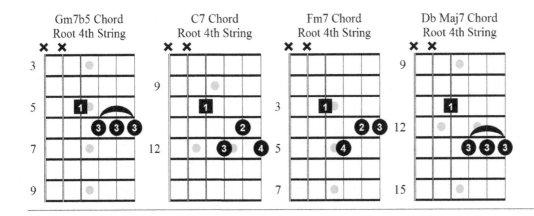

Try playing the same chord sequence just using these chords. This example may be a little more difficult as you may not be as familiar with the note names on the 4th string as you are with the 5th and 6th strings. Take your time and persevere.

Example 2e:

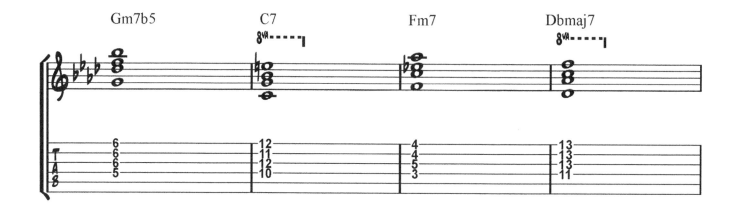

As before, these chords jump up and down the neck a lot, so we can combine them with 5th string chords to make them flow more easily.

Try beginning the chord sequence on a 5th string Gm7b5 and then move to a 4th string C7.

Example 2f:

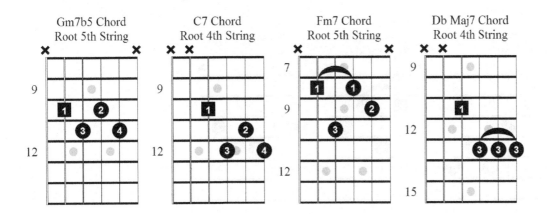

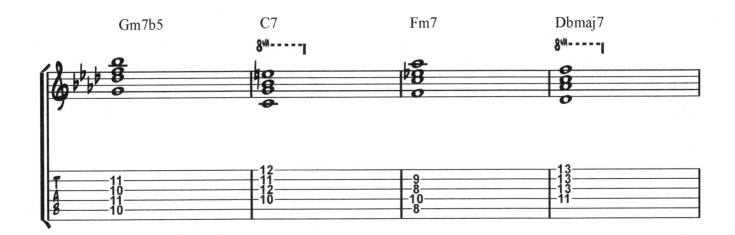

We could also change the chord voicing we use for the final Dbmaj7 in this sequence. If we play it as a 6th string root chord, the voicings will flow together more smoothly:

Example 2g:

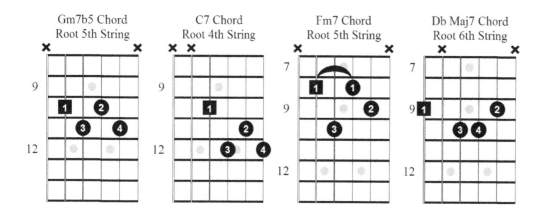

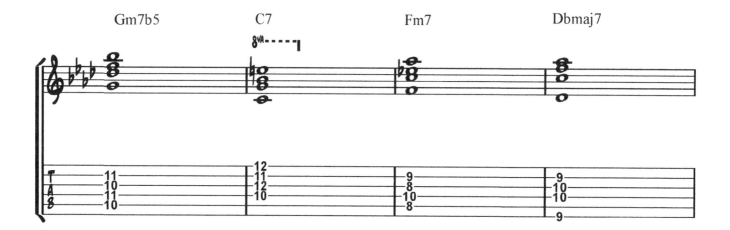

Try starting the chord sequence on different strings and see how closely you can voicelead the chord progression. Here is just one possible 'route' through the changes starting on the 6th string:

Example 2h:

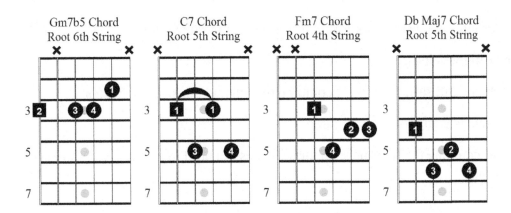

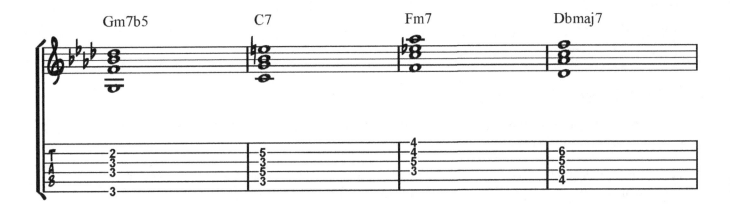

Now you are comfortable with the common voicings of these essential jazz chords, find as many ways as you can through the following chord progressions using the voicings discussed in this chapter:

1)

2)

Begin by playing through each progression using chords all with roots on the same string.

Next, combine the 6th and 5th string voicings.

When you are confident with 6th and 5th string voicings, combine the 4th and 5th string voicings.

Finally find the closest chord voicings using roots on all three strings.

In this chapter, you have learnt to combine the four most important types of chord in jazz in a common jazz chord progression. These chords are :

Major 7

Minor 7

Dominant 7

and

Minor 7b5 (m7b5)

By learning each root position chord in combination with other chords that are commonly played together, you're not just learning 'shapes', you're learning music.

These chord types can be used to get through 80% of all jazz tunes. They have been given in *root position*, in other words, they are played with the root (tonic) note played as the bass (lowest) note of the chord.

Later, when we study other types of voicings, you will see that it is not necessacery (and often not desirable) to play the root note in the bass, and we can create *inversions* of a chord by placing the 3rd, 5th or 7th note of the chord in the bass.

The best way to practice jazz chords to apply them to real songs, and there are plenty of ways to do this.

If you've picked up this book, there's a good chance you're interested in lerning some jazz *standards* (early jazz songs) and it is easy to get a hold of some. The traditional way is to buy a "Real Book", which is like a bible of jazz tunes. Each chord *chart* contains the melody (or *head)* and is written above the chords for the tune.

The Real Book is a *big* book and contains hundreds of tunes you'll probably never learn fully, but are great to practice with. These hundreds of tunes contain multiple combinations of chords and sequences. You can open it on a random page and simple play through the chords in the song. You'll start to recognise sequences that crop up time and time again ,and find new ways to navigate them on your guitar.

Playing through chord charts with a metronome is one of the best ways to learn to *comp* jazz chords. The metronome is important as you will learn to stay in time and play at a constant rate. If you make a mistake, don't worry, just stay in time and get the next chord right. If there is a really difficult passage, switch the metronome off and plan your route through the chords.

While there are thousands of jazz songs, only around a few hundred are commnly known. Of those few hundred, most jazz players normally like to play only around 20 to 30 of their favourites.

These favorite songs are common at jazz jam nights and so it is wise to start your jazz playing career by learning the chords (and melody) to some of the most popular tunes.

Learning 20 or 30 songs is a big task but there is no hurry. Focus on learning one at a time and do everything you can to memorise it. This is a lot easier if you see it in terms of the four chord types given above.

Jazz standards are often grouped into tunes that have similar chord changes. For example, you might hear Autumn Leaves described as a "ii V I" tune because it contains lots of ii V I chord progressions.

Tunes like Anthropology and Oleo are grouped as "Rhythm Changes" tunes, beacause they are based on the changes to George Gershwin's I Got Rhythm.

We will talk about different types of chord progression in the next chapter.

It is useful to know what "type" of progression each standard is, as they are often used as workhourse tunes when learning to solo and there is a list of the most popular jazz standards and their types of progression in the next chapter.

One tip; if you don't want to buy a Real Book, is to do a Google image search for the title of the standard you want to learn, and add the word "chart".

For example, you can find the chord changes to the Miles Davis tune, Seven Steps to Heaven, by searching "Seven Steps to Heaven Chart" and then clicking "Images".

Chapter Three: Ten Essential Jazz Chord Progressions

As I mentioned at the end of the previous chapter, most jazz players like to focus on playing around 20 to 30 jazz standards. If another tune comes up at a jam night or as a request at a gig, normally their skills developed by learning their existing repertoire will allow them to play the new tune fairly easily.

This is because the "core" of jazz standards are built around many of the same common chord progressions. In fact, in my book **Chord Tone Soloing for Jazz Guitar,** I break these common progressions down into just 13 fundamental chord sequences. The most common of these are given below.

When you have learnt the following chord progressions in many different keys, you will quickly discover that they come up time and time again in the most common jazz standards. Think of each of the following sequences as a little 'unit' that can be combined to build complete songs.

I hope this makes the mystical world of jazz music suddenly a lot more tangible. All those crazy chord progressions can be broken down into just a few common sequences that are combined in different ways.

The following are all in the key of Bb, but transpose them to different keys and play them around The Circle of Fifths cyclic exercises which we touch on at the end of the book.

ii V I Major

Example 3a:

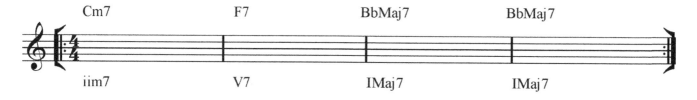

The Major ii V I progression is the bedrock on which jazz is formed. It can be heard in almost every tune from the late swing period onwards. It is important to know that in jazz, the iim7 chord was a slightly later addition and found more popularity during the bebop period. In the majority of the swing era, this chord progression was normally written as simply V I. The ii chord was added by bebop players to provide additional soloing options without affecting the tonality of the progression.

Good 'workhorse' tunes that feature the major ii V I sequence are:

- Blue Bossa
- Tune Up
- Autumn Leaves
- Perdido
- All the Things You Are

Example 3b:

I vi ii V7

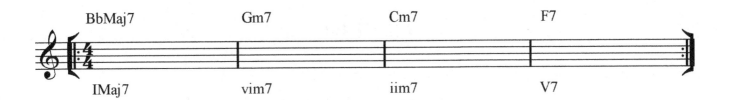

The I vi ii V progression is extremely common in jazz and is featured in many jazz standards. The sequence was popularised by George Gershwin with the tune, I Got Rhythm and has been a jazz staple ever since. While you will often see it played in its original form, as shown above, the *quality* of each chord is often changed. The quality of the chord is whether it is Maj7, m7, or 7, etc. For example, it is fairly common in jazz to hear each in the sequence chord played as a dominant 7 voicing.

The I vi ii V progression is known as a *turnaround* chord sequence because it is often found at the end of a chord progression and turns the song around back to the start.

You will come across the I vi ii V progression time and time again in jazz, and some useful tunes to study are:

- I Got Rhythm
- Oleo
- Moose the Mooche
- Isn't It Romantic?
- Heart and Soul

Example 3c:

I7 VI7 II7 V7

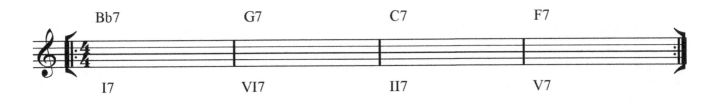

The previous *diatonic* I vi ii V progression frequently occurs in jazz and forms the basis for many popular standards. However, some of the chords in this progression are often altered and given different *qualities*.

The quality of a chord is the part after the root note that *describes* its mood and construction. For example, a chord's quality could be Maj7, m7, m7b5, 7, 7b9 or even something like 13#9.

In jazz, *any* chord can have its quality changed, and the most common alteration is to make some chords into dominant 7s. In the I vi ii V progression, the vi chord (Gm7 in the above progression) will often be played as a dominant 7 chord (G7). Even the I chord is sometimes changed to become a dominant 7 to create a bluesy effect.

Example 3d:

I (ii V7 I) i

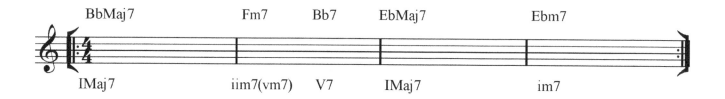

This chord sequence combines two essential progressions into one exercise. The first three bars can be viewed as a key change (modulation) from Bb to Eb Major, or simply as a decorated chord I to IV movement. If you have ever played a blues, you will know how important the I-IV chord progression is. In a blues, however, chords I and IV both are normally played as dominant 7 chords.

- Satin Doll
- Cherokee
- Joy Spring
- Have You Met Miss Jones?
- There Will Never Be Another You

In bar four, the new tonic chord (EbMaj7) becomes Ebm7. Again, this kind of movement occurs frequently in jazz.

Example 3e:

I (i V I)

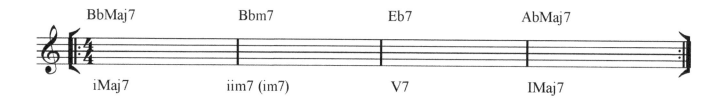

This progression has quite a lot in common with one previous. A Maj7 (BbMaj7) chord becomes a m7 (Bbm7) chord, which is now the first chord of a Major ii V I progression in a new key.

This type of chord movement is extremely common in jazz, and a useful way to modulate to a new key.

The Major to minor movement occurs in many jazz tunes including:

- How High the Moon
- Tune Up
- Cherokee
- One Note Samba
- Solar

Example 3f:

I II7 iim7 V

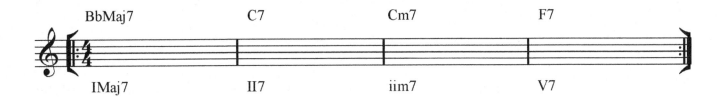

This sequence crops up surprisingly regularly and has a recognisable feel. It often occurs in Latin music, especially in the work of Antônio Carlos Jobim.

This chord sequence, when viewed from bar three onwards forms a ii V I in Bb Major, although, in bar two, there is a dominant version of the iim7 chord.

This chord sequence occurs in many tunes, including:

- Take the 'A' Train
- Donna Lee
- The Girl from Ipanema
- Desafinado
- Mood Indigo

Example 3g:

I7 IV7 V7 IV7

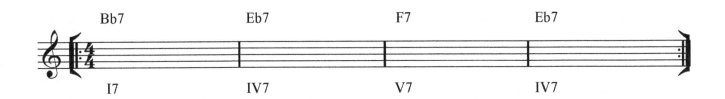

You can think of this sequence as a 'distilled' 12 bar blues.

Popular jazz blues tunes include:

- Billie's Bounce
- C Jam Blues
- Au Privave
- Straight No Chaser

Example 3h:

ii V I Minor

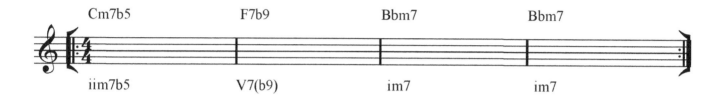

The minor ii V i progression is extremely common and occurs in many tunes. It functions as a musical 'full stop' in much the same way as the Major ii V I.

For much more information and study of the minor ii V i check out my book **Minor ii V Mastery for Guitar.**

Tunes that extensively feature the minor ii V i sequence include:

- Alone Together
- Summertime
- Softly, as in a Morning Sunrise
- Beautiful Love
- Autumn Leaves

Example 3i:

The Minor Blues

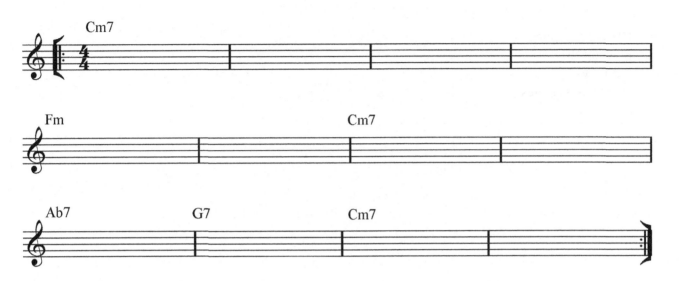

The minor blues is one of the most frequently played jazz progressions and is an especially common request at jam nights. Normally played at a high tempo, this 12 bar blues progression differs from the 'standard' jazz blues because of its minor key centre, and the relative simplicity of its harmony.

As you can see, there are long periods of static chords, and most of the harmonic interest is generated in bar nine by the non-diatonic Ab7.

Jazz tunes that use the minor blues structure include:

- Mr PC
- Equinox
- Blue Train
- Israel

Example 3j:

Descending ii Vs

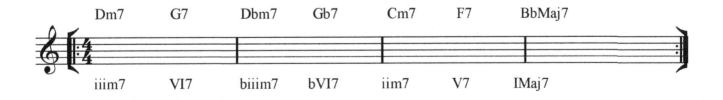

This is one of the trickier sequences in jazz. A series of chromatically descending ii Vs are played that begin from chord iii of the eventual resolution point of Bb Major.

It should be noted that this kind of descending chord sequence can begin at any point in a tune, and not necessarily resolve to the tonic key. For example, bar four of the above progression could quite easily be Bm7, Fm7 or even Gbm7.

This type of descending sequence is a big feature of a 'Charlie Parker-style' blues, and can be heard in tunes such as:

- Blues for Alice
- Four on Six
- Satin Doll
- West Coast Blues

Chapter Four: Root and Guide Tone Voicings

The 3rd and 7th intervals of any chord are called the *guide tones.*

Even without the root, it is possible to almost perfectly define *any* chord sound by playing just its 3rd and 7th. You will learn later that two related dominant chords can share the same set of guide tones, but for now we can define almost any chord by its root, 3rd and 7th.

To recap,

Chord Type	Interval Formula
Major 7	1 3 5 7
Dominant 7	1 3 5 b7
Minor 7	1 b3 5 b7
Minor 7b5	1 b3 b5 b7

A slight complication arises with the minor 7b5 chord because it has the same guide tones intervals (b3 and b7) as a minor 7 chord. This is not a problem because although they *share* the same guide tones, by playing just the b3 and b7 we do not define whether the 5th is natural or flattened. In other words, we are not adding any extra information and the guide tones sound fine whether the chord is m7 or m7b5. Other instruments in the band can play the b5 and the listeners' ears are very good at filling in the missing information.

We will begin by examining a fretboard diagram with a root note of C marked, and the b3, 3, b7 and 7 highlighted.

Guide Tones from
a 6th String Root

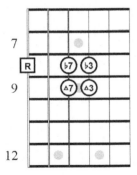

Remember, the root note played together with the 3rd or 7th, define the most important tones in any chord.

To play a Maj7 chord, you play root, 3rd and 7th. To play a Dominant 7 chord, you play root, 3 and b7.

Example 4a:

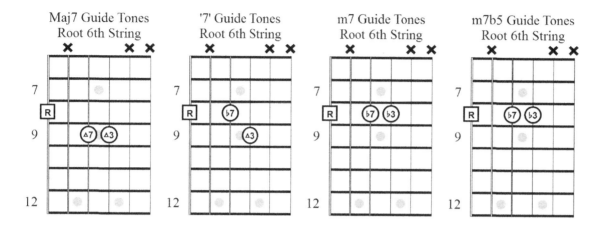

Play through the diagrams above and listen to the effect that changing only one note has on each voicing. Can you hear the qualities of each chord being described by just these three pitches?

Of course, the m7 and m7b5 chords share the same guide tones as mentioned before. Don't worry about this, but if you are desperate to hear the guide tone voicing with the added b5, you can play the following chord:

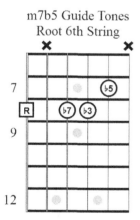

Play through this progression using just the root and guide tone voicings based on the 6th string.

You can hear it in **example 4b:**

Gm7b5   C7   Fm7   Dbmaj7

Now let's look at root and guide tone voicings with a 5th string root.

Here is the fretboard overview:

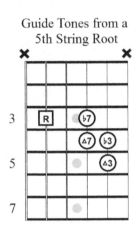

And here are the root and guide tone voicings for each chord.

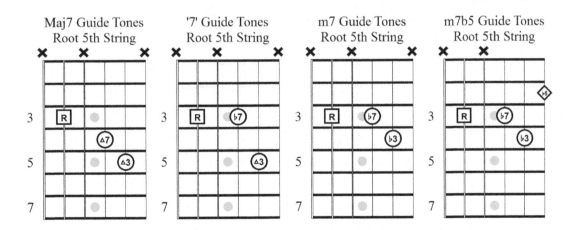

Once again, in the m7b5 diagram, the b5 is **not** a guide tone and is optional. For now you should ignore it.

Play through the following progression just using root and guide tone voicings on the 5th string:

Gm7b5   C7   Fm7   Dbmaj7

In this position, the 3rds in each chord can be played on the fourth string, one octave lower. By playing the 3rd on the fourth string, we create the following map of guide tones:

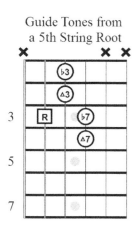

This means that the 5th string root and guide tone chords can be played:

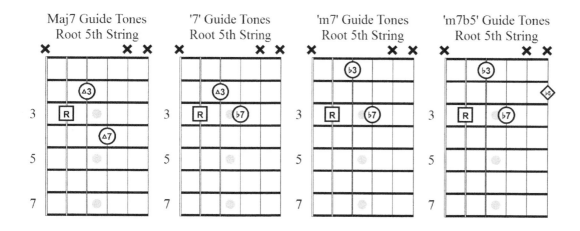

Now, let's combine the root and guide tone voicings from both the 6th and 5th string roots and play through the same sequence in a much smoother movement:

Example 4c:

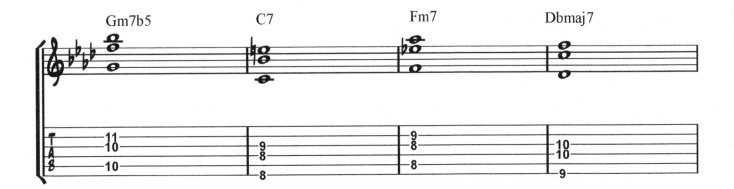

Try this approach starting on the 6th string also:

Example 4d:

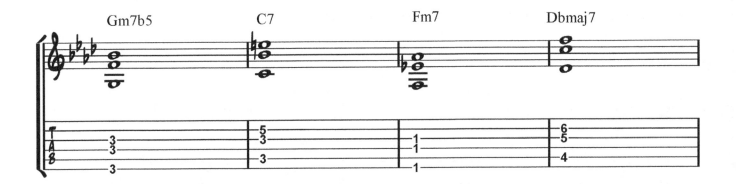

Or

Example 4e:

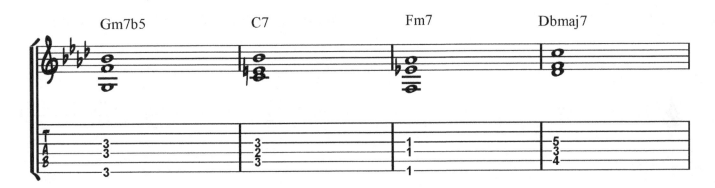

Listen to the difference between using different voicings of the root and guide tones. The voicings with the 3rd on the second string tend to be a little brighter than the ones with the 3rd on the fourth string.

Finally, we can learn the guide tone voicings with a root on the fourth string:

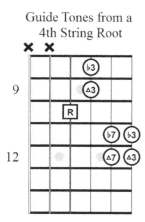

As you can see, once again there are two options as to where we voice the 3rd, either on the third string or on the first string. They're both good voicings but playing the 3rd on the first string creates slightly easier fingerings. Experiment to find your favourite sounds and voicings.

The four chord types can be voiced with a fourth string root in the following ways:

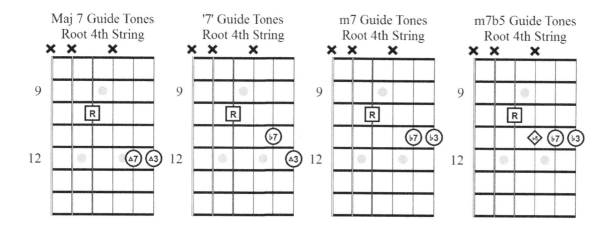

Play through the same chord sequence using the guide tone voicings with their roots on the 4th string:

Gm7b5   C7   Fm7   Dbmaj7

Now try combining 4th string and 5th string roots. Here is one possible route through the changes:

Example 4f:

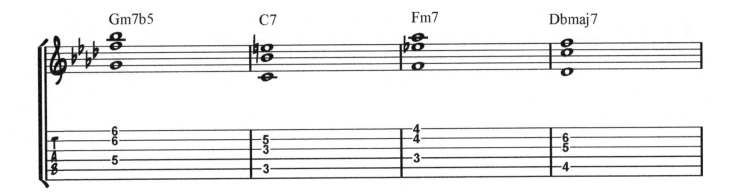

Finally, try combining all three string groups and find as many routes through the changes as you can. Here is one beginning from the 4th string.

Example 4g:

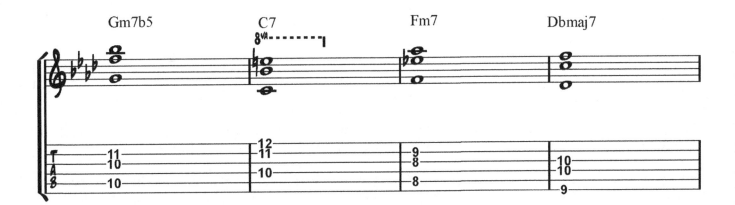

Try the same approach with the following progressions:

1)

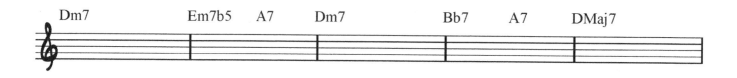

2)

3)

Apply guide tone voicings to all chord sequences at the end of the previous chapter. Don't forget to try them in different keys and use the exercises at the end of the book to help you become fluent.

Root and guide tone voicings are extremely useful when *comping* (strumming) jazz guitar rhythm, especially when you're playing with a bigger band or any lineup where there is a piano. Pianos and horn sections can often provide a great deal of harmonic information, and by overplaying on the guitar we can often clash with them unless parts are worked out quite carefully.

By playing root and guide tone voicings we are playing just the basic (yet important) chord information and we can focus more on providing a musical, rhythmic accompaniment to the ensemble. The guitar was, after all, traditionally used as a rhythm insturment, not a melodic one.

Chapter Five: Drop 2 Voicings

Drop 2 voicings are some of the most widely used, versatile chord voicings used in modern music. They are not instrument specific and can be played on any harmonic instrument or 'shared' between a horn, brass or string section.

In this section, we will play all the chords on top four strings as this is the most common way to play drop 2 chords.

m7 Drop 2 Voicings

We will begin by learning the four voicings for a drop 2 Fm7 chord. Pay very careful attention to where the root notes (squares) are in the following diagrams. By knowing where the root notes are, you will find it is much easier to transpose these chords into other keys later.

I mentioned earlier that we don't always need to play the root note as the bass (lowest) note in a chord. The four chords below are a perfect example of this.

You know that any '7th-type' chord is made up from four notes, R, 3, 5 and 7.

If the root is in the bass, then this is called a 'root position' chord.

If the 3rd is in the bass, this is called a 'first inversion' chord.

If the 5th is in the bass, this is a 'second inversion' chord.

If the 7th is in the bass, this is a 'third inversion' chord.

Right now, it is only important that you understand that the four notes of the chord can be played with different intervals in the bass.

Example 5a:

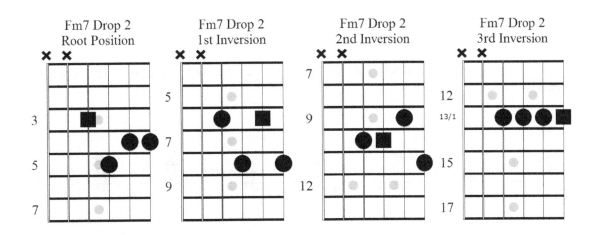

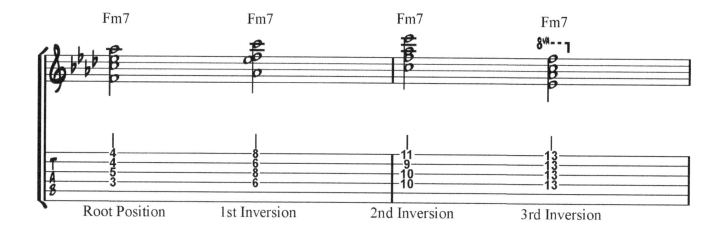

Begin by playing slowly through the four inversions of Fm7. The final voicing can be played at either the thirteenth or first fret.

To help you memorise the shapes, practice the following ideas over backing track 1. Don't worry too much about playing in a regular rhythm, just work on smoothly transitioning between the four shapes.

Ascend and descend through the four voicings. **Example 5b:**

1) Practicing moving between pairs of chords, for example between the root and first or the first and second inversions of Fm7. **Example 5c:**

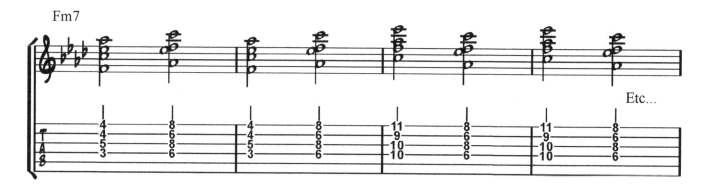

2) Try skipping inversions by playing root – second then first to fourth inversions.

Example 5d:

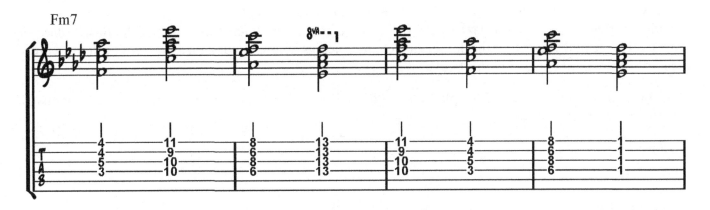

Finally, try simply jamming along with backing track one and playing these voicings whenever you like.

As mentioned previously, the key to applying these chords musically is to always know where the root note is in each voicing. The following diagram shows where all the F notes are located on the top four strings.

Learn the voicings in the context of these root notes.

F Root Notes

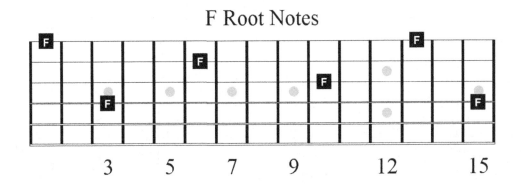

A useful tip is to listen to great piano players like Bill Evans, Keith Jarrett, and Bud Powell and listen to how they phrase chords rhythmically, especially while 'comping' under the solos of other musicians.

Dominant 7 Drop 2 Voicings

Now we will explore the inversions of the C7 drop 2 chord voiced on the top four strings. The dominant 7 chord is extremely common in jazz and is often altered with *chromatic tensions* (which we will discuss later). It is essential you master the dominant 7 chord voicings before moving on as we will be doing a great deal of work with them later in this book.

The four, drop 2 voicings for C7 are played as follows. Remember to pay great attention to the locations of the root notes in each shape.

Example 5e:

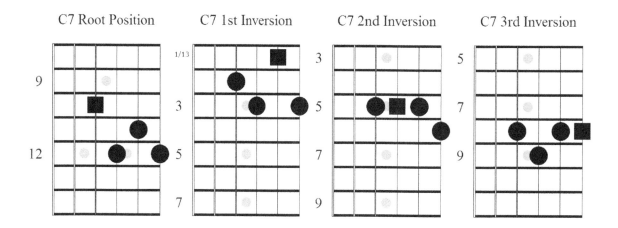

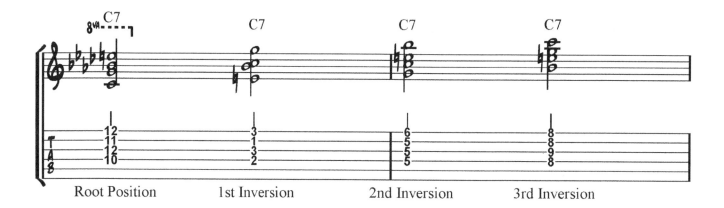

Playing these chords from low to high on the guitar neck gives us the following.

Example 5f:

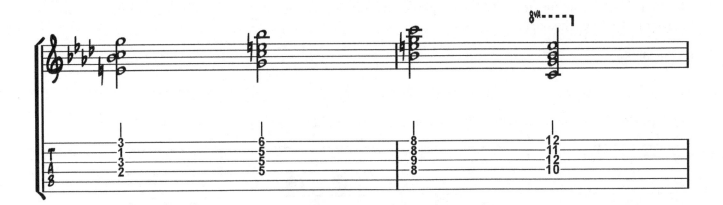

Repeat the steps in chapter two to memorise and use these voicings.

1) Ascend through the voicings from lowest to the highest.
2) Descend through the voicings from highest to lowest.
3) Move between pairs of chords, gradually ascending or descending the fretboard.
4) Skip chords and play alternate voicings ascending and descending the neck.
5) Jam along with Backing Track 2, a static C7 groove.

Minor 7b5 Drop 2 Voicings

We have now studied both the m7 and dominant 7 drop 2 chords in the key of F minor. To extend the progression we will add in the ii chord, Gm7b5. Now we can form the important minor ii V i progression.

The four drop 2 voicings for Gm7b5 are played as follows. Remember to pay attention to the locations of the root notes in each shape.

Example 5g:

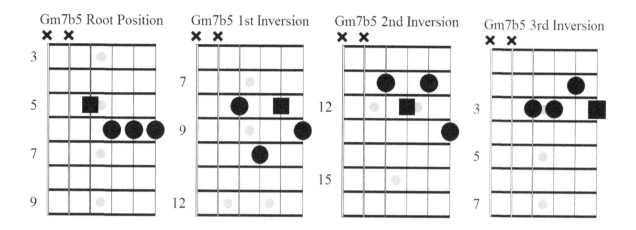

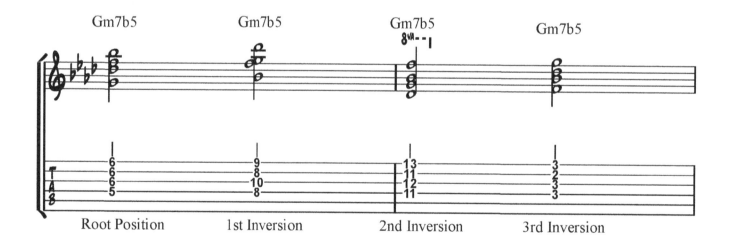

Repeat the following steps in order to memorise and internalise the sound of these voicings.

1) Ascend through the voicings from lowest to the highest.
2) Descend through the voicings from highest to lowest.
3) Move between pairs of chords, gradually ascending or descending the fretboard.
4) Skip chords and play alternate voicings ascending and descending the neck.
5) Jam along with Backing Track3, a static Gm7b5 groove.

When you are feeling more confident with the bass line connections, try playing the m7b5 voicings with root notes of Eb, C, Bb and Db.

To reinforce these m7b5 chord voicings and to put them into a musical context, we will now learn them in conjunction with the C7 and Fm7 chords from the previous two sections.

You may remember that one of the best ways to practice these chords is by finding the smallest movement possible between the chord changes. As you already mastered moving from C7 to Fm7 in the previous chapter, adding in the Gm7 to form a full minor ii V i shouldn't take too long.

To save space, the following four chord sequences are combined into one line of notation below.

Example 5h:

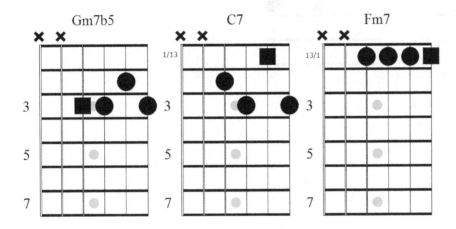

Example 5i:

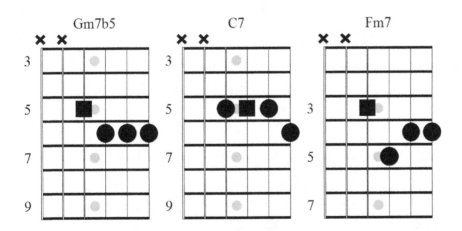

Example 5j:

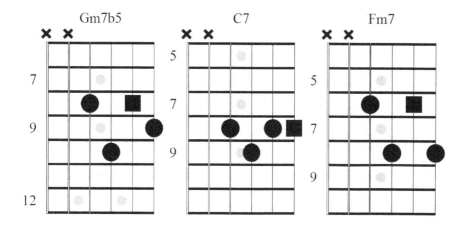

Example 5k:

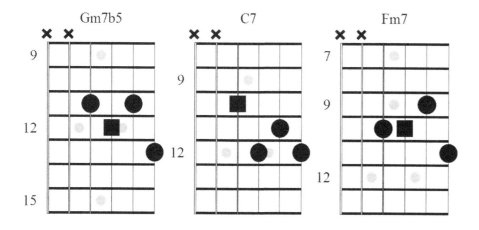

Examples 5h – 5k:

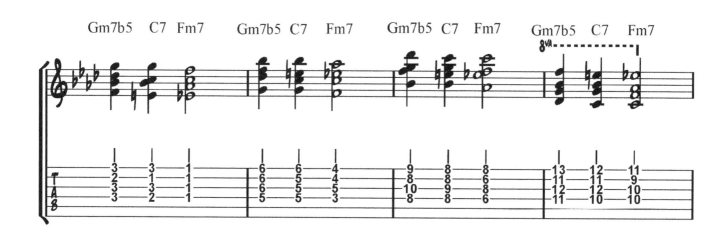

These ideas are extremely effective when descending the neck:

Example 5l:

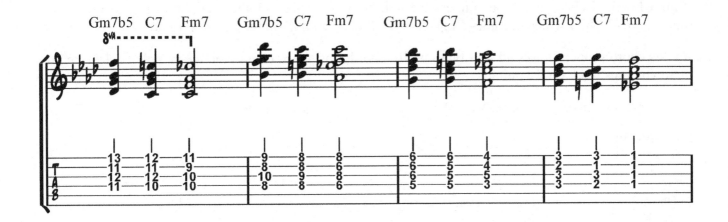

Major Seventh Drop 2 Voicings

The final chord quality we need to examine is the Maj7 chord. Continuing to work in the key of F minor, there is a major 7th chord on the sixth degree of the scale; DbMaj7.

With a DbMaj7 chord under our fingers we will be able to play another common musical progression: iim7b5 - V - I - bVI which becomes Gm7b5 - C7 - Fm7 - DbMaj7 in the key of F minor.

As this chord sequence uses all four types of 7th chord, it is an excellent practice vehicle for learning how these voicings work on the guitar.

The four drop 2 inversions of DbMaj7 that you need to know are as follows.

Example 5m:

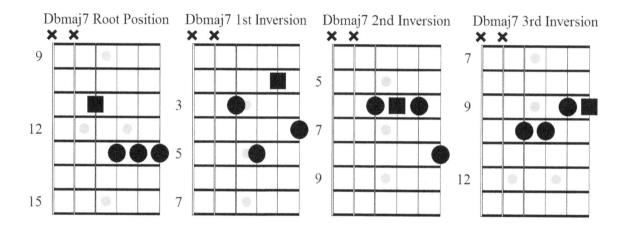

These can be arranged from low to high on the guitar neck in the following way.

Example 5n:

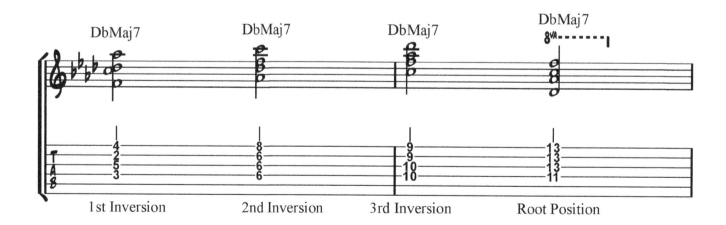

As always, repeat the following steps to memorise and internalise the sound of these voicings.

Ascend through the voicings from lowest to the highest.

1) Descend through the voicings from highest to lowest.
2) Move between pairs of chords, gradually ascending or descending the fretboard.
3) Skip chords and play alternate voicings ascending and descending the neck.
4) Jam along with Backing Track 4, a static DbMaj7 groove.

Begin by finding the closest possible way to move between these chords in each position on the neck. The following examples are combined in one line of notation below the diagrams to save space.

Example 5o:

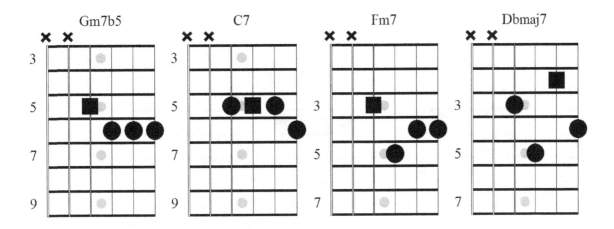

Example 5p:

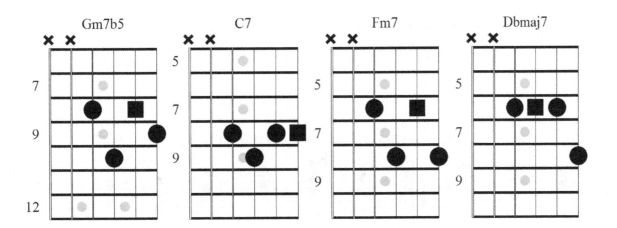

Example 5q:

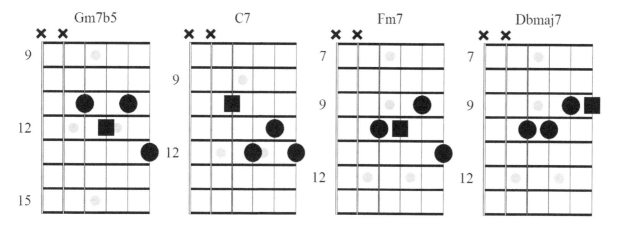

Example 5r:

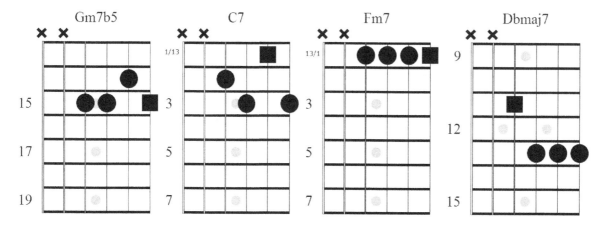

Try these sequences ascending and descending the guitar neck. You can also practice ideas where you make the melody note on the first string ascend or descend on every chord change.

Example 5s:

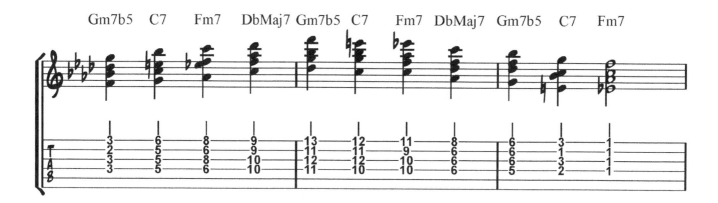

Go back and apply all these drop 2 chord voicings and inversions to the chord sequences given in Chapter Three. This will take some time, but your chord knowledge will increase massively.

Chapter Six Extensions and Alterations to Dominant Chords

Diatonic Extensions to Dominant 7 Chords

In jazz, it is common to add diatonic 'extensions' and chromatic 'alterations' to dominant 7 chords. A natural or 'diatonic' extension is a note that is added to the basic 1 3 5 b7 chord, but lies within the original parent scale of the dominant chord. In other words, to form an extended dominant chord we continue skipping notes in the scale, just as we did when we originally learnt to form a chord.

We can extend the basic 1 3 5 b7 chord formula to include the 9th, 11th and 13th scale tones.

These extensions occur when we extend a scale beyond the first octave. For example, here is the parent scale of a C7 chord (C Mixolydian):

C	D	E	F	G	A	Bb	C	D	E	F	G	A	Bb	C
1	2	3	4	5	6	b7	1/8	9	3	11	5	13	b7	1

Notice that in the second octave, the original chord tones still referred to as 1, 3, 5, or b7. This is because the function of these notes never changes in the chord: A 3rd will always define whether a chord is major or minor and the b7 will always be an essential part of a m7 or 7 chord.

The notes *between* the chord tones are the notes that have changed their names. Instead of 2, 4 and 6, they are now 9, 11, and 13. These are called *compound* intervals

In very simple terms a C13 chord could contain *all* the intervals up until the 13th:

1 3 5 b7 9 11 and 13 – C E G Bb D F and A

In practice though, these are a huge amount of notes (we only have six strings), and playing that many notes at the same time produces an extremely heavy, undesirable sound because many of the notes will clash with one another.

The answer to this problem is to remove some of the notes from the chord, but how do we know which ones?

There are no set rules about which notes to leave out in an extended chord, however there *are* some guidelines about how to define a chord sound and what *does* need to be included.

To define a chord as major or minor, you must include some kind of 3rd.

To define a chord as dominant 7, major 7 or minor 7, you must include some kind of 7th.

As you know, these notes, the 3rds and 7ths are called guide tones, and they are the most essential notes in any chord. These notes are more important than even the root of the chord and quite often in jazz playing, the root of the chord is dropped entirely in favour of a richer extension such as the 9th.

Let's examine common ways to play the extensions that regularly occur on dominant chords in jazz progressions.

To name a dominant chord, we always look to the highest extension that is included, so if the notes were 1, 3, b7 and 13 we would call this a dominant 13, or just '13' chord. Notice that it doesn't include the 5th, the 9th or the 11th but it is still called a '13' chord.

As long as we have the 3rd and b7th a chord will always be a dominant voicing.

We will begin by looking at this fairly common voicing of a D7 chord. In the following example, each *interval* of the chord is labelled in the diagram.

In D7 the intervals 1 3 5 b7 are the notes D, F#, A and C.

Example 6a:

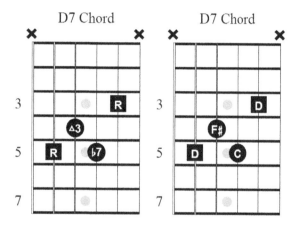

The 'triangle 3' symbol is musical shorthand for 'major 3rd'.

As you can see, this voicing of D7 doesn't include the 5th of the chord (A).

Here is the extended scale of D Mixolydian (the parent scale of D7).

D	E	F#	G	A	B	C	D	E	F#	G	A	B	C	D
1	2	3	4	5	6	b7	1/8	9	3	11	5	13	b7	1

We can use this voicing of D7 to form a dominant 9 or '9' chord. All we need to do is add the 9th of the scale (E) to the chord. The easiest way to do this is to move the higher-octave root (D) up by one tone and replace it with an E.

Example 6b:

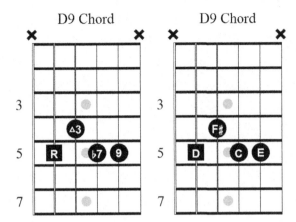

Look carefully to make sure you understand how I replaced the root of the chord with the 9th of the chord to form a dominant 9 or '9' chord. All I did was to move the root note on the 2nd string up by a tone.

The intervals contained in this chord voicing are now 1, 3, b7 and 9. We have the 3 and b7 defining the chord as dominant and the 9th (E) creating the *extended* dominant 9th chord.

Dominant 11th or '11' chords are less common and need some special care because the essential major 3rd of (F#) can easily clash with the 11th (G).

The most common way to voice an 11 chord it to lower the 5th of a dominant chord by a tone to become an 11th (4th up an octave). The 11th is generally voiced one octave above the 3rd otherwise a semitone clash between the 3rd and 11th can occur.

Here is one voicing of a D7 chord, this time it does contain the 5th:

Example 6c:

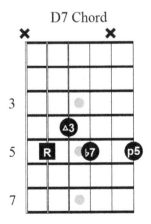

By lowering the 5th (A) by a tone to the 11th (G) we form a dominant 11 or '11' chord.

Example 6d:

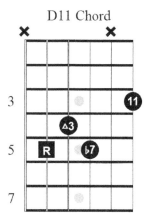

D11 Chord

This voicing is very useful to know as '11' chords do crop up from time to time and it's useful to have a stock chord *grip* that will get you through the tune.

Dominant 13 chords are much more common than dominant 11 chords. They are normally created by raising the 5th of a dominant 7 chord by one tone to become the 13th (6th up an octave). It is common to include the 9th of the scale in a 13th chord, but it is by no means necessary.

By combining the last two ideas we can form a D9 chord with the fifth on the 1st string of the guitar:

Example 6e:

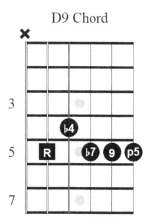

D9 Chord

By raising the 5th by a tone we can reach the 13th degree (interval) of the scale. The chord is given first with the intervals shown, and then with the recommended fingering:

Example 6f:

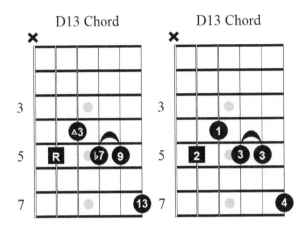

As I'm sure you're starting to see, adding extensions to dominant chords is simply a case of knowing where the desired extension is located on the fretboard and then adjusting a non-essential chord tone to that location.

The above 13 chord can also be voiced slightly differently to achieve a subtly different flavour. In the next example we replace the 9th with the 3rd:

Example 6g:

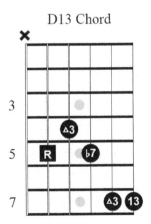

In this voicing there are two 3rd which is completely acceptable but you will probably find the preceding version with the 9th included to be a slightly richer sound.

This adjustment approach can be applied to dominant 7 chords voiced with a 6th string root. Here are the guide tones of a D7 chord with a 6th string root:

Example 6h:

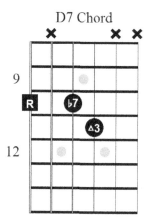

The 5th and higher octave root of this chord are located here:

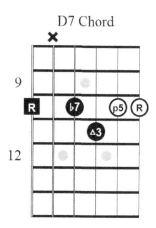

If you remember, we can raise the 5th by a tone to play the 13th of the chord, and we can raise the root of the chord by a tone to target the 9th.

Example 6i:

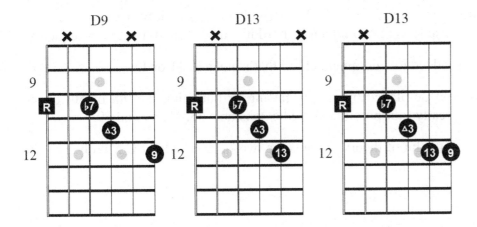

The third diagram shows a 13 chord which includes the 9th. It is still a 13th chord whether or not the 9th is present.

The following two 'shell' voicings are extremely useful fingerings to know, as it is easy to add extensions to them while keeping the root of the chord in the bass. However, as you will learn later, diatonic extensions are often added by the clever use of chord *substitutions* that completely replace the original chord.

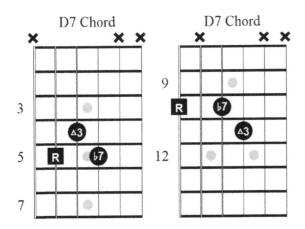

Chromatic Alterations to Dominant Chords

While diatonic extensions (9, 11 and 13) are often added to a dominant chord, it is also extremely common to add *altered* or *chromatic* extensions to a dominant chord. These alterations mainly occur at points of musical tension in a chord progression, such as the dominant 7 chord in a ii V7 I (two, five, one) sequence.

A chromatic alteration is a note that is added to a dominant chord that is not a 9, 11 or 13.

Every possible chromatic alteration can be played by simply raising or flattening the 9th or 5th of the dominant chord, in fact there are only really four possible altered extensions; b5, #5, b9 and #9.

To see why this is true, let's look at a little bit of theory. Here is the two-octave scale of C Mixolydian, the parent scale of C7:

C	D	E	F	G	A	Bb	C	D	E	F	G	A	Bb	C
1	2	3	4	5	6	b7	1/8	9	3	11	5	13	b7	1

And here it is laid out on the guitar neck:

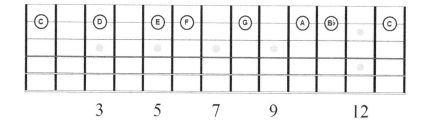

The 5th of the C scale is the note G, and the 9th is the note D.

I can sharpen the 5th (G) to become a G# to create a #5 tension.

I could create the same result by flattening the 6th or 13th note (A) to become an Ab/G#.

A b13 interval is exactly the same as a #5. The chords C7#5 and C7b13 are pretty much the same depending on who you talk to. Some would say that C7b13 may contain a natural 5th because it isn't specifically shown in the chord symbol that the 5th is altered. In other words, it *may* contain both the natural 5th *and* the b13... but this is extremely unlikely and not worth worrying about!

If you look at the fretboard again, you will see that a #11 (F#) is identical to a b5 (Gb).

A similar thing happens with the 9th of the scale however in any dominant chord you would *never* flatten the 3rd because it would change the quality of the chord from dominant to minor 7.

Remember dominant = 1 3 5 b7, and minor 7 = 1 b3 5 b7. By flattening the 3rd of a dominant chord we have changed the chord quality and it is no longer dominant, unless there is another major 3rd sounding in the chord.

I can sharpen the 9th (D) to become a D# and create a C7#9 sound. I can also flatten the 9th to Db to create a 7b9 sound. The C7#9 sound will still contain a major 3rd even though it will clast with the #9 interval.

It is acceptable to remove the root note from any chord and possible to raise the root by a semitone to create a b9 sound.

We cannot raise the b7 of the chord because it would change the chord quality from dominant 7 to major 7.

In summary: b5 = #11 and #5 = b13 so the only true altered extensions to a dominant chord are b5, #5, b9 and #9. You will see chords written down like C7#11b13. This isn't wrong, it's just a question of terminology. The key is to realise that C7#11b13 is the same as C7b5#5.

The reason I teach b5, #5, b9, #9 is because it makes the chords much easier to understand and play on the fretboard.

Working with a D7 chord, here is a fretboard diagram showing the 1 3 b7 shell voicing of a dominant chord in black, and the 5th and 9th intervals marked in white:

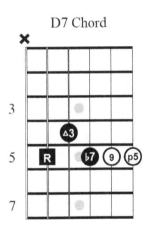

D7 Chord

I can create *any* altered extension by simply moving the white notes up or down by one semitone.

Example 6j:

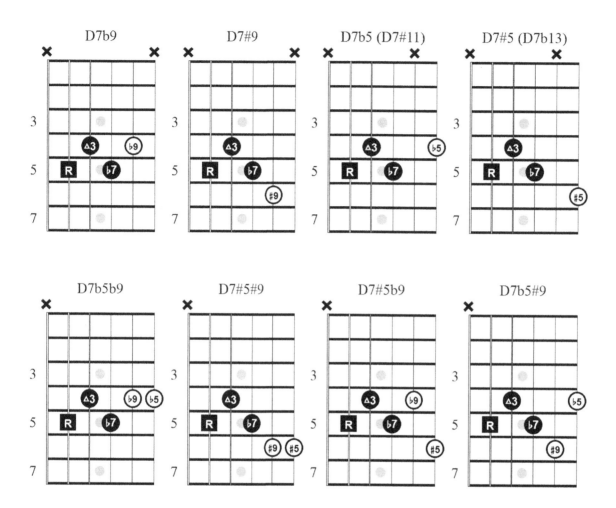

The same is true when we use the dominant 7 shell voicing with a root on the 6th string:

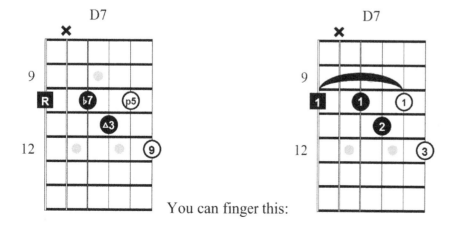

You can finger this:

Some of the altered extensions in this position can be a little hard to reach so quite often these voicings are played rootless. Here are a few of the altered extension permutations available in this position.

Example 6k:

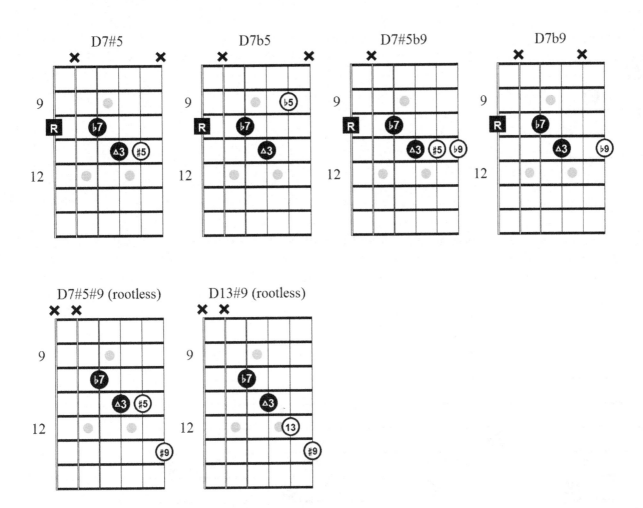

These approaches can be used with a dominant 7 chord with the root on the 4th string too, although in the basic root position voicing we learnt earlier, we must omit the root when adding a #9 or b9.

The following example uses a G7 chord as the basis for the alterations.

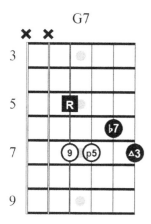

The easiest alterations in this position are the #5 and b5, although often the root note will be raised a semitone to create a rootless 7b9 chord.

Example 6l:

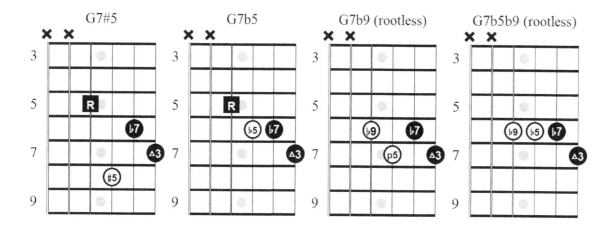

Quite often in jazz chord charts you will simply see the symbol 'alt'. For example 'D7alt'. This means that the composer has not specified a particular altered extension for a dominant 7 chord, and so you can use whichever one you feel works best with the music.

It is also important to know that just because a chord chart says '7' it doesn't mean that the chord must be played as a 'straight' 7 chord. If the dominant chord is *static* (not moving), it is normally fine to add in as many natural extensions as you like. For example, four bars of D7 could be played like this:

Example 6m:

D13   D9   D13   D7

If a dominant 7 chord is *functional* (resolving to another chord) then a basic '7' chord can normally be substituted for any dominant chord with a natural extension *or* chromatic alteration.

A chord progression like this where the (functional) D7 resolves to the GMaj7 already has tension on the D7:

Example 6n:

Am7   D7   GMaj7   E7

Jazz musicians are happy to add *any* amount of altered tension to a functional dominant chord, so they may play it any or more of the following ways:

Example 6o:

Am7   D7b9   GMaj7   E7#5b9

Example 6p:

Am7   D7b5b9   GMaj7   E7#5#9

Example 6q:

Am7   D9   GMaj7   E7b5#9

Try playing through the following examples beginning from different root notes, and substitute any diatonic or chromatic extensions you like for the dominant chords you have learnt already.

1)

Dm7   G7   CMaj7   Dbm7b5

2)

Cm7   Em7b5   BbMaj7   G7

3)

B7 (altered)   E7 (alt)   A7 (alt)   D7 (alt)   GMaj7

We can take the same approach when adding chromatic alterations to major 7, minor 7 and m7b5 chords, the secret is simply to know where the alterations are on the fretboard.

Chapter Seven: Diatonic Extensions to Other Chord Types

Chord types other than dominants can be extended. The folllowing section will teach you voicings for the most common chords you will come across. Remember, all these chords can be 'simplified' back to their original 7th form, i.e. you can play a Bbm11 as a Bm7 if you want to.

Diatonic Extensions to m7 Chords

Minor 7 chords (1 b3 5 b7) are most commonly extended to just 9ths and 11ths voicings.

The following diagrams show the most common 'Root Position' shapes used to play them on the guitar.

Example 7a:

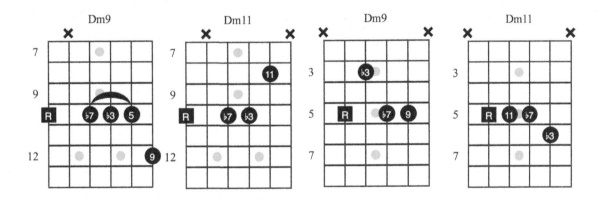

Diatonic Extensions to Maj7 Chords

Major 7 chords (1 3 5 7) are most commonly extended to just Major 9ths, although the Major7#11 chord isn't too uncommon in more modern settings. In fact, the fourth chord of the major scale naturally harmonises to Maj7#11 so this can be used to imply a Lydian sound.

The following diagrams show the most common 'Root Position' shapes used to play them on the guitar.

Example 7b:

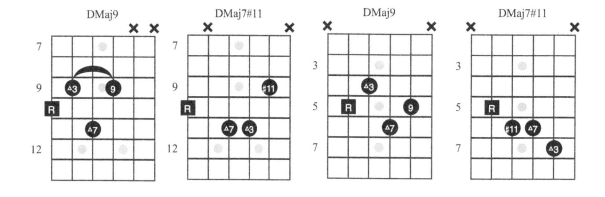

Diatonic Extensions to m7b5 Chords

Minor 7b7 chords (1 b3 5b b7) are normally only extended to natural 9ths, however the diatonic m7b5 chord that exists on the 7th degree of the major scale actually extends to m7b5b9.

This concept is a bit complicated could probably fill a book all by itself, but m7b5b9 chords are very rarely used and they are very 'crunchy'. Instead, jazz musicians tend to opt to play the more harmonious m7b9 most of the time.

If in doubt, just play a m7b5. It'll be fine.

The following diagrams show the most common 'Root Position' shapes used to play m9b5 chords on the guitar. Notice that they don't contain a m3rd. The listeners' ears will fill in the gaps.

Example 7c:

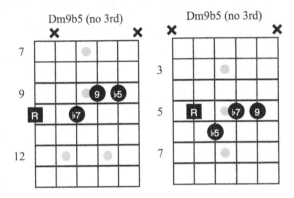

Chapter Eight: Diminished 7 Chords

Now we have looked at how the most common four 7th chords are formed and played we will take a look at some structures that fall slightly outside the system we have been using so far. The chords in the following chapters are all very common occurrences in jazz.

We will begin with the diminished 7 chord.

As you learnt at the start of this book, a diminished triad consists of the scale intervals 1 b3 b5. A diminished 7 chord adds a *bb7* (double flat 7) interval to this triad to give the formula

1 b3 b5 bb7.

In the key of C this formula generates the notes C Eb Gb Bbb (A).

The diminished 7 chord occurs naturally when you harmonise the 7th degree of the harmonic minor scale.

While the bb7 is *enharmonically* the same note as the 6th, this structure is always seen as a 7th voicing.

When laid out on the fretboard, you will notice that the notes of a diminished chord have an unusual quality.

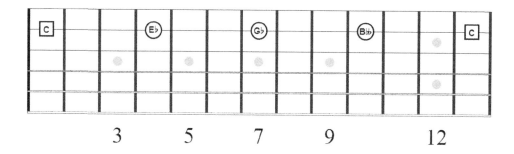

Each note is a minor 3rd (one-and-a-half tones) apart. This has some far-reaching theoretical consequences but for now it is important to realise just one thing:

The notes in the chords of C Dim7, Eb Dim7, Gb Dim7 and A Dim 7 are the same. This symmetry leads to some interesting possibilities in terms of modulation.

Diminished chords have an instantly recognisable sound, and are commonly heard in old-fashioned horror movies and in the music of J.S. Bach!

You can fret diminished 7 chords with roots on the 6th, 5th and 4th strings.

Example 8a:

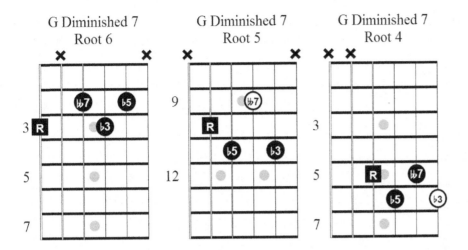

To create a classic Hammer-Horror sound, try moving a diminished 7 chord up or down by the interval of a minor 3rd:

Example 8b:

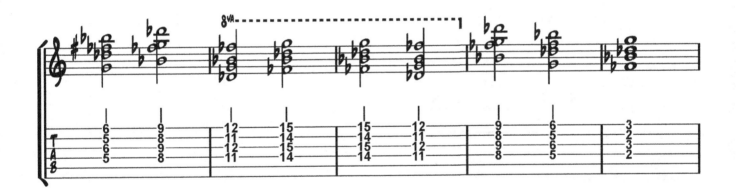

Try it with each of the three chord voicings above.

The "Diminished" Substitution

The diminished chord is often as a sound in its own right, it is commonly used as a *substitution* for other chords.

Compare the chords of C7 and C# diminished 7:

Example 8c:

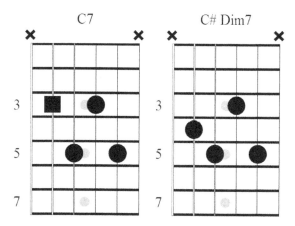

You can see that the chord of C# diminished contains *exactly* the same notes as C7, *apart from the root*, which has been raised by a semitone to become a b9 interval.

You can see this in the following diagram of intervals.

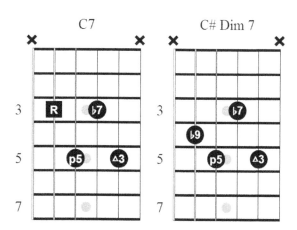

A C# diminished chord contains exactly the same notes as a *rootless* C7b9 chord. This concept teaches us one of the most common substitutions in jazz.

Even though I taught you this substitution as playing a C#Dim7 chord instead of a C7 chord, jazz musicians tend see this substitution as building a diminished 7 chord on the *3rd* of a dominant chord. Remember, diminished 7 chords are symmetrical so C# diminished 7 contains the same notes as the following chords:

C# Dim7 – **E Dim7** – G Dim7 – Bb Dim7.

It is normally easier to see a chord substitution built on a chord tone like the 3rd, as opposed to a non-chord tone like the b9, even though they are technically the same thing.

This substitution works beautifully, and can be used every time you encounter a functional dominant chord.

All you need to do to create a 7b9 sound is play a dim7 chord on the 3rd of the original dominant chord.

For example, in the chord progression

You can substitute the chord E Dim7 (or C#Dim7) for the C7 chord to create a C7b9:

Example 8d:

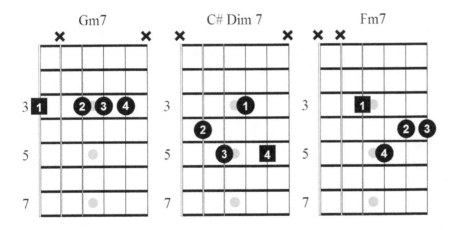

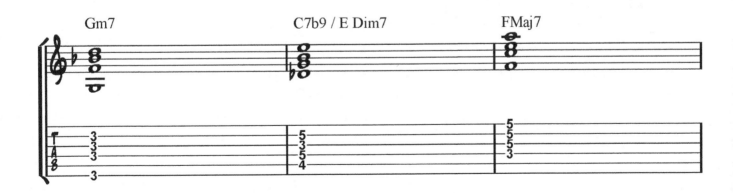

Because of its symmetrical nature, there is no reason you can't use more than one diminished substitution on the C7 chord. Try moving the diminished chord up by three frets before resolving to the FMaj7 chord:

Example 8e:

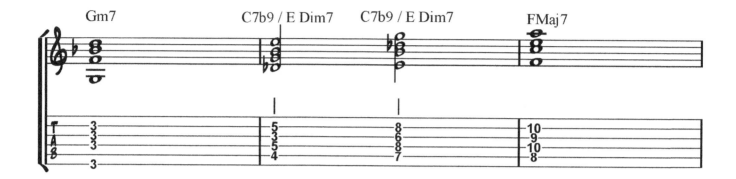

As long as you play with good rhythm, you can play as many voicings of the diminished 7 substitution as you like in place of the original dominant 7 chord.

This is normally the first chord substitution that jazz musicians learn as it gives instant access to an altered dominant sound. It is also easy to remember and sounds fantastic.

The diminished 7 chord can be a little difficult to finger at first. One tip for the voicings on the 5th and 6th strings is to develop your finger dexterity by first fretting a dominant 7 chord and then quickly altering it to the dim 7 fingering. For example, try moving between the following fingerings:

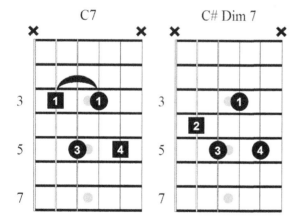

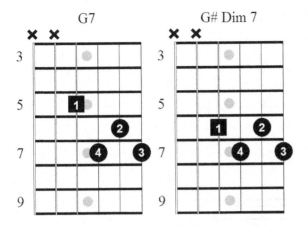

I would recommend fretting the 6th-string dim 7 chord with the following fingering:

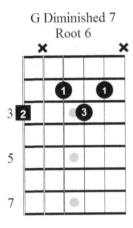

G Diminished 7
Root 6

One common use of the diminished 7 chord is in bar six of a jazz blues:

Example 8f:

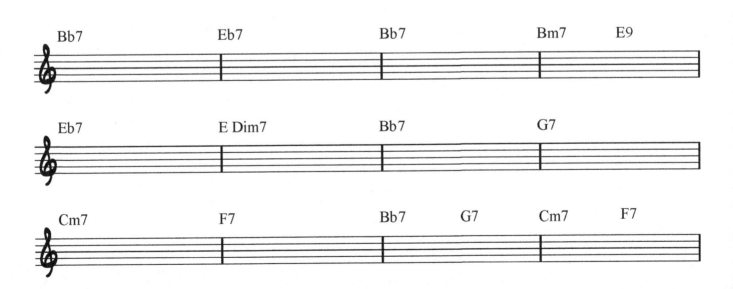

Using the E Dim 7 chord in bar six has the effect of creating an Eb7b9 chord which adds some tension before resolving back to the Bb root of the progression.

Try using a diminished substitution for each of the dominant 7 chords in the final two bars of previous progression.

Instead of:

Play a dim 7 chord on the 3rd (or b9) of each 7 chord:

Practice this diminished substitution with voicings based off the 6th, 5th and 4th strings.

Remember the following rule: "Any functional dominant chord can be replaced with a diminished chord built on the 3rd to create a 7b9 sound."

Chapter Nine: Major and Minor 6 Chords

Major and minor 6 chords are often used in many types of music, especially in early-era jazz. They are extremely useful to know.

Major 6 chords have the formula 1 3 5 6.

Minor 6 chords have the formula 1 b3 5 6.

In modal contexts, you may occasionally need to play a b6 on a minor chord although that is fairly uncommon.

Major 6 chords

There are two ways to think about major 6 chords, either as the triad (1 3 5) with the added 6 or as a major7 chord where the 7th has been lowered by a tone. Both approaches are useful.

Major 6 chords are often seen notated as simply '6' or 'M6' for example C6 or CM6 although the former would be more common.

You can play major 6 chords with roots on the 6th, 5th and 4th strings in the following ways:

Example 9a:

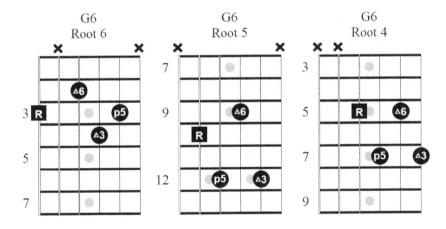

Examine the following diagrams and you will see why a major 6 chord can be thought of as a major 7th with the 7th lowered by a tone:

Example 9b:

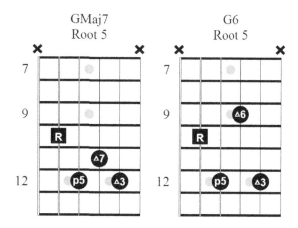

Major 6 chords are fairly bright-sounding and are normally used as a direct substitution for a major or major 7-type chord.

For example, in the chord sequence

Example 9c:

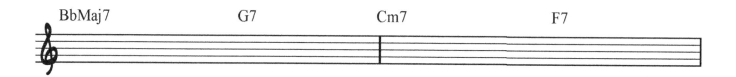

you could certainly play the following.

Example 9d:

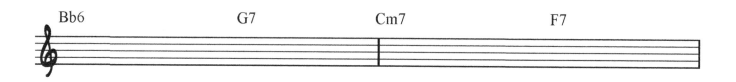

Although many older chord charts state major 6, a more modern approach would be to replace the major 6 chord with a major 7th.

Minor 6 Chords

Minor 6 chords have the formula 1 b3 5 6. They can be seen as a minor triad (1 b3 5) with an added 6, or as a minor 7 chord with the 7th lowered by a semitone. In the key of C the formula 1 b3 5 6 generates the notes C Eb G A.

Minor 6 chords are often used directly in place of m7 chords but sometimes the use of a m6 chord has some subtle implications when soloing.

Minor 6 chords can be voiced from the 6th, 5th and 4th strings in the following ways.

(Key of G)

Example 9e:

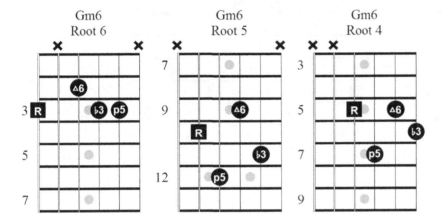

The following diagram shows that a m6 chord can be seen as a m7 chord with the b7 lowered by a semitone:

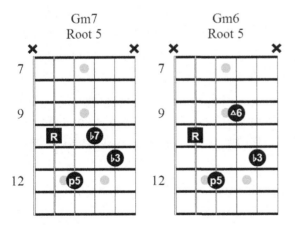

The following progression is one of the most common in which a minor 6 chord is used. Notice the minor/Major7 chord? This is a m7 chord where the b7 has been replaced with a natural 7 (1 b3 5 7). It's not a common sound, but you'll hear it in tunes like My Funny Valentine.

Example 9f:

This sequence can be played:

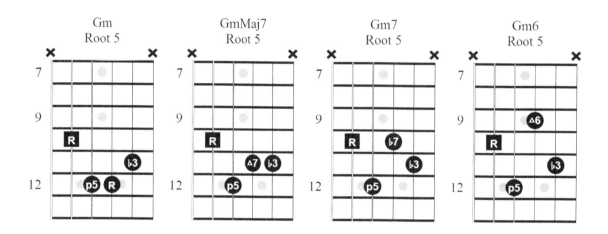

As you can see, the root of the chord (on the 3rd string) descends by a semitone with each chord change.

If you see a m6 chord on a chord chart it is normally there for a specific reason, either the melody note of the tune is a 6th, or more likely the chart is telling you that this chord is the tonic chord in a *melodic minor* progression.

Without wading too deeply into music theory, the tonic (I) chord of a melodic minor scale harmonises to become a minMaj7 (pronounced "Minor Major 7th") chord. It is a *minor* chord with a *major* 7th and has the formula 1 b3 5 7. This is somewhat of a 'tense' chord and not really as stable a sound as you might look for in a 'home' chord.

Minor/Major 7ths are great chords, but they do have a very particular flavour which is not always appropriate for a minor ballad as you heard in the previous example. Often, a composer's solution is to replace the tonic mMaj7 with a m6. (Although for a great use of a mMaj7 chord as a tonic, check out Miles Davis' version of Solar)

If you're soloing and you see a m6 chord, a good first choice scale is often melodic minor.

Chapter Ten: Diatonic Chord Substitution

Until this point in the book we have generally been selecting specific intervals to form particular types of chords. In this chapter we will look in more depth at the idea of diatonic substitutions.

A 'diatonic' substitution is one where the *substitute chord* originates from the *same key* or harmonised scale as the *original chord*.

The most common use of this principle is to build chords with natural extensions by continually 'stacking' intervals above a bass note.

For example, let's take the scale of C Major:

C	D	E	F	G	A	B	C	D	E	F	G	A	B	C
(1)	2	(3)	4	(5)	6	(7)	1	(9)	3	(11)	5	(13)	7	1

We know we can build a CMaj7 chord in the following way:

1 3 5 7 (C E G B)

A CMaj9 chord that contains *every note* is formed with

1 3 5 7 9 (C E G B D).

A CMaj11 chord is formed with

1 3 5 7 9 11 (C E G B D F).

And a CMaj13 chord is formed with

1 3 5 7 9 11 13 (C E G B D F A).

As previously discussed, we do normally include every note in these extended chords so we often discard less important intervals like the 5th and the root when constructing them.

Another way to reach the higher extensions of a chord is to use a substitution. By building a new 7th chord from one of the chord tones of the original chord we can reach 'upper structures' (extensions) easily and use chord forms we already know to imply a richer, extended chord sound.

Look at the notes in CMaj9: C E G B D.

If we get rid of the root (C), we are left with the notes E G B D. These notes form an Em7 chord.

By playing an Em7 chord over a bass note of C we create a CMaj9 sound.

The following example shows this concept played on the guitar. The root (C) is included just for your reference. The Em7 chord is shown in black dots and the intervals as they relate to the root note of C are given.

Example 10a:

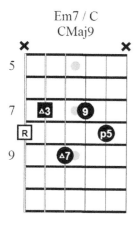

By simply playing an Em7 chord in place of a CMaj7 chord we have created a CMaj9 sound. The note C is not played in this voicing. This is often desirable as other instruments, such as the bass, will normally be playing it.

The rule is that we can always play a m7 chord on the 3rd of a Maj7 chord to create a Maj9th chord.

In fact, we can use some kind of '7th' chord built on the 3rd of any other 7th chord to extend it up to the 9th.

If we know the harmonised major scale, we can simply 'jump a 3rd' to find out which 7th chord to use as a substitution. Here is the harmonised scale of C Major.

I	ii	iii	IV	V	vi	vii
CMaj7	Dm7	Em7	FMaj7	G7	Am7	Bm7b5

In the previous example, we used chord iii (Em7) as a substitution to form a rootless CMaj9 chord.

Interval from C	1	3	5	7	9
CMaj7	C	E	G	B	
Em7		E	G	B	D

Now, let's form a Dm9 chord in the same way.

Interval from D	1	b3	5	7	9
Dm7	D	F	A	C	
FMaj7		F	A	C	E

This can be viewed on the guitar in the following manner:

Example 10b:

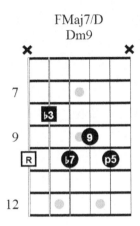

Building a Maj7 chord on the b3rd of a minor 7 chord creates a rootless m9 chord.

The same process can be used to build a dominant 9 chord.

To form a dominant 9 chord, we can play a *m7b5* chord of the 3rd of a dominant 7 chord.

Putting this into the key of C, we can use the Bm7b5 chord to imply a rootless G9 sound.

Interval from G	1	3	5	b7	9
G7	G	B	D	F	
Bm7b5		B	D	F	A

On the guitar this looks like:

Example 10c:

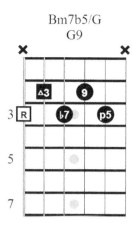

Finally, to create a *m7b5b9* sound, we can play a m7 chord on the b3 of the original m7b5 chord.

In the key of C this would mean playing a Dm7 chord over Bm7b5.

Interval from B	1	b3	b5	b7	b9
Bm7b5	B	D	F	A	
Dm7		D	F	A	C

Example 10d:

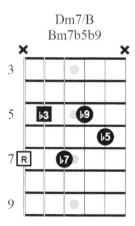

Every substitute chord in this context is taken from the harmonised major scale. When each of the degrees of the major scale are harmonised we generate the following sequence of chords.

This may seem like a lot of rules, but because these examples derive from the harmonised major scale (which always harmonises in the same way) these rules are constant. In other words, to form a Maj9 sound, you can *always* play a m7th on the 3rd.

Here is a summary of the last few pages:

Original Chord Type	Substitution on the 3rd	Rootless Extended Chord
Maj7	m7	Maj9
m7	Maj7	m9
7	m7b5	9
m7b5	m7	m7b5b9

To test yourself, work out which chord could you build on the 3rd of the following chords to form a '9th' voicing.[1]

    1) FMaj7
    2) EMaj7
    3) Gm7
    4) Bbm7
    5) F7
    6) A7
    7) Gm7b5
    8) Dm7b5

---

[1] 1) Am7, 2) G#m7, 3) BMaj7, 4) Dbmaj7, 5) Am7b5, 6) C#m7b5, 7) Bbm7, 8) Fm7

Using Diatonic Substitutions

Diatonic substitutions built on the 5th and the 7th of a chord are a lot less common than substitutions built on the 3rd. This is because if we create an extension to a chord by playing a 7th chord on the 5th, we lose both the root *and* the 3rd. The 3rd is an important note so these extensions (that would result in an '11th-type' extension, are less common.

When we build a 7th substitution from the 3rd we're really just replacing the root with the 9th. As you've heard throughout this book, the 9th is a very acceptable extension and can be used almost anywhere.

Try playing through the following progression using Backing Track 5.

Example 10e:

This time, build a 9th chord on the Cm7 chord by using a substitution on the b3.

The notes of Cm7 are C Eb G Bb

So you can use chord EbMaj7 to create a Cm9 sound.

Play the progression again over backing track one, but this time substitute EbMaj7 for the Cm7 chord.

Example 10f:

Repeat the exercise, but this time use the substitution on the F7 chord. To create a '9' sound we play a m7b5 chord on the 3rd.

Example 10g:

Finally, repeat the process but this time build a BbMaj9th. To create a Maj9 sound we can play a m7 chord on the 3rd.

Example 10h:

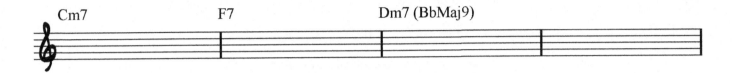

As you are playing these substitutions with a strong bassline on the backing track, it is easy to hear how the substitution functions to build a 9th on each chord.

If you have a strong rhythm section or backing track you can normally add in as many 9th substitutions as you like. However, if you are playing as a duo and accompanying a singer, you may need to be careful with these ideas as most vocalists need to hear the root of the chord.

Try combining the three substitutions above:

Example 10i:

Try this with and without the backing track and notice how the context of the chords changes. Over the backing track you'll normally hear the 9th extension fairly easily, without the backing track you may just hear the substitution chord until your ears get used to filling in the missing root note.

Chapter Eleven: Practice Tunes

The following chord progressions are taken from extremely common jazz tunes. You can use each one as a workhorse to help you apply all the concepts from this book.

Here is a suggested set of chord ideas to practice:

1) Learn the chords with roots on just the 6th string of the guitar.

2) Learn the chords with roots on just the 5th string of the guitar.

3) Combine chords with roots on 6th and 5th strings of the guitar.

4) Learn the chords with roots on the 4th string of the guitar.

5) Combine chords with roots on 5th and 4th strings of the guitar

6) Combine chords across 6th, 5th and 4th strings.

7) Play chords using drop 2 chords (top four strings) in just the 0 to 4th fret area.

8) Play chords using drop 2 chords (top four strings) in just the 3rd to 7th fret area.

9) Play chords using drop 2 chords (top four strings) in just the 6th to 10th fret area.

10) Play chords using drop 2 chords (top four strings) in just the 9th to 13th fret area.

11) Use 6th, 5th and 4th string chords, but play each functional (resolving) dominant chord as a 7b9 by using the diminished substitution. (i.e., play a Dim7 chord on the 3rd of the dominant E.g., ADim7 instead of F7)

12) Replace all m7 chords with m9 chords

13) Replace all m7 chords with m11 chords

14) Play every Maj7 chord as a Maj9 by substituting a m7 chord on the 3rd (E.g., Dm7/BbMaj7)

15) Play every m7 chord as a m9 by substituting a Maj7 chord on the b3rd (E.g., DbMaj7/Bbm7)

16) Play every 7 chord as a 9 chord by substituting a m7b5 chord on the 3rd (E.g., Dm7b5 / Bb7)

17) Combine steps 12 – 16 to your taste

18) Play drop 2 voicings as above, but use the diminished substitution on every functional dominant chord. (Remember, you can just raise the root by a semitone)

19) Replace every functional (resolving) dominant chord with a 7#9 chord

20) Replace every functional (resolving) dominant chord with a 7#5 chord

21) Replace every non-functional (static) dominant chord with a 9 chord

22) Replace every non-functional (static) dominant chord with an 11 chord

23) Replace every non-functional (static) dominant chord with a 13 chord

24) Play all Maj7 chords as Maj6 chords and all m7 chords a m6 chords

Jazz Blues - E.g., Billie's Bounce:

Billie's Bounce

(Medium Up Swing)   Charlie Parker

$\begin{array}{llll} \frac{4}{4} F_7 & | B^\flat_7 & | F_7 & | C_{m7} \ F_7 \ | \\ | B^\flat_7 & | B_{o7} & | F_7 & | A_{m7} \ D_7 \ | \\ | G_{m7} & | C_7 & | F_7 \ D_7 & | G_{m7} \ C_7 \ \| \end{array}$

ii V I Tune - E.g., Autumn Leaves

Autumn Leaves

(Medium Swing)   Joseph Kosma

A
$\frac{4}{4} C_{m7} \quad | F_7 \quad | B^\flat_{\Delta7} \quad | E^\flat_{\Delta7} \quad |$

$| A_{ø7} \quad | D_7 \quad | G_{m7} \quad | \ /\! . \ \}$

B
$| A_{ø7} \quad | D_{7\sharp5} \quad | G_{m6} \quad | \ /\! . \ |$

$| C_{m7} \quad | F_7 \quad | B^\flat_{\Delta7} \quad | E^\flat_{\Delta7} \quad \|$

C
$| A_{ø7} \quad | D_7 \quad | G_{m7} \ G^\flat_7 \ | F_{m7} \ E_7 \ |$

$| A_{ø7} \quad | D_7 \quad | G_{m6} \quad | \ /\! . \ \|$

Rhythm Changes - E.g., Oleo

Oleo

(Up Tempo Swing)   Sonny Rollins

A

$\begin{array}{c}4\\4\end{array}$ $\|:$ B$\flat_{\Delta7}$ G$_7$ | C$_{m7}$ F$_7$ | D$_{m7}$ G$_7$ | C$_{m7}$ F$_7$ |

| F$_{m7}$ B$\flat_7$ | E$\flat_7$ A$\flat_7$ | $\overline{1.}$ D$_{m7}$ G$_7$ | C$_{m7}$ F$_7$:$\|$

$\overline{2.}$ | C$_{m7}$ F$_7$ | B$\flat_6$ | $\|$

B

$\|$ D$_7$ | $\%$ | G$_7$ | $\%$ |

| C$_7$ | $\%$ | F$_7$ | $\%$ $\|$

A

$\|$ B$\flat_{\Delta7}$ G$_7$ | C$_{m7}$ F$_7$ | D$_{m7}$ G$_7$ | C$_{m7}$ F$_7$ |

| F$_{m7}$ B$\flat_7$ | E$\flat_7$ A$\flat_7$ | C$_{m7}$ F$_7$ | B$\flat_6$ | $\|$

Minor ii V I Tune E.g., Alone together

Alone Together

(Medium Swing)   Arthur Schwartz

A
$\frac{4}{4}$ || D$_{m6}$ | E$_{ø7}$ A$_{7♭9}$ | D$_{m6}$ || E$_{ø7}$ A$_{7♭9}$ |

| D$_{m6}$ | A$_{ø7}$ D$_{7♭9}$ | G$_{m7}$ | ∕. |

| B$_{m7}$ E$_7$ | G$_{m7}$ C$_7$ | F$_{Δ7}$ | E$_{ø7}$ A$_{7♭9}$ |

1.   E$_{ø7}$ A$_{7♭9}$ 2.
| D$_{Δ7}$ | ∕. :|| D$_{Δ7}$ | ∕. ||

B
|| A$_{ø7}$ | D$_{7♭9}$ | G$_{m6}$ | ∕. |

| G$_{ø7}$ | C$_{7♭9}$ | F$_{Δ7}$ | E$_{ø7}$ A$_{7♭9}$ ||

A
| D$_{m6}$ | E$_{ø7}$ A$_{7♭9}$ | D$_{m6}$ | E$_{ø7}$ A$_{7♭9}$ |

| D$_{m6}$ B$_{ø7}$ | B♭$_7$ A$_{7♭9}$ | D$_{m6}$ | E$_{ø7}$ A$_{7♭9}$ ||

ii V I Tune (Bossa) E.g., Blue Bossa

Blue Bossa

(Bossa Nova)   Kenny Dorham

$\frac{4}{4}$ || C$_{m7}$ | ∕. | F$_{m7}$ | ∕. |

| D$_{ø7}$ | G$_{7♭9}$ | C$_{m7}$ | ∕. |

| E♭$_{m7}$ | A♭$_7$ | D♭$_{Δ7}$ | ∕. |

| D$_{ø7}$ | G$_{7♭9}$ | C$_{m7}$ | D$_{ø7}$ G$_{7♭9}$ ||

Chapter Twelve: Cyclic Exercises in 12 keys

The cyclic chord progressions in this section are very useful when it comes to practicing chord voicings.

One way to use them is to pick a chord structure and quality, for example, a drop 2 m7 chord. Now limit your playing to a small, five or six fret area of the guitar such as the first to sixth fret.

Play around each cycle using that chord structure and quality but do not allow yourself to leave the set area on the fretboard. Using the cycle of fourths chart below, you would play drop 2 voicings of the following chords: Cm7, Fm7, Bbm7, Ebm7 etc. Try the same idea with the cycle of fifths: Cm7, Dm7, Am7 etc. Practice this concept with any chord structures you are studying.

You can also use each chord in the cycle as a *tonic chord*. For example, you could play major ii V I progressions into each chord in turn. Using the cycle of fourths, you would play a ii V I *into* **C** (Dm7 G7 CMaj7), **then** a ii V I *into* **F** (Gm7 C7 FMaj7) **then** a ii V I *into* **Bb** (Cm7 F7 BbMaj7) etc.

These kinds of exercises are mentally demanding because they make you think *backwards* from a target tonic chord. Memorising the chord sequence in advance away from the guitar can really help before attempting these cyclic exercises.

These practice techniques are very powerful, and with discipline you will find that your vision, knowledge and above all your *ears* will improve dramatically.

Cycle of Fourths

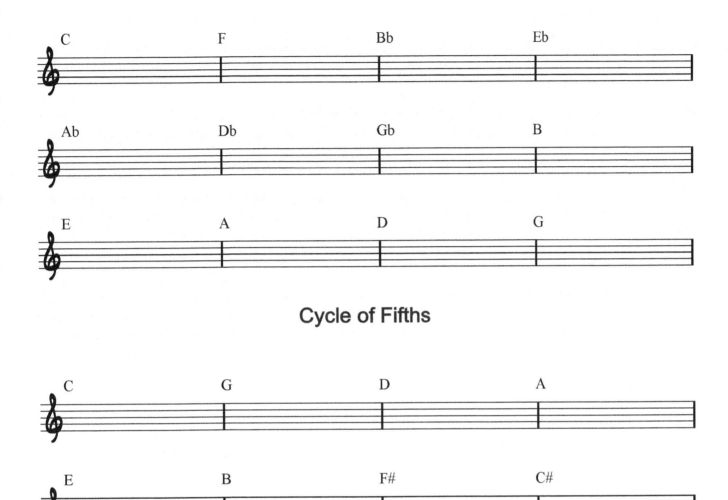

Cycle of Fifths

For much more information on how you can use the circle of fifths to improve your playing, check out my book **The Circle of Fifths for Guitarists**.

Conclusions and Further Reading

Congratulations; You made it!

Getting through this book is no mean feat. There has been a huge amount of information given and if you've worked through the chapters methodically, you should be well on your way to playing virtually any jazz guitar chord chart put in front of you.

If you still occasionally see a chord that you're not immediately sure how to deal with (don't worry, it happens to the best of us!) then remember that most chords can be reduced to just one of four types.

As one great teacher once said to me, "If in doubt, play the letters, not the numbers!"

I've done my best to cover 99% of all jazz chord eventualities, so at the bare minimum you should be able to make it through most tunes convincingly. However, as you can probably guess, the world of jazz chords is a bit of a rabbit hole...

So, where to next?

Well, the best thing you can do is get in a band and play jazz. This is your quickest route to success. There's nothing like learning on your feet in the rehearsal room or on stage to internalise all this knowledge. You'll find things you didn't know existed, and, when you get back to your practice room later, you can analyse the theory of why it worked.

If you want to dive headfirst into the rabbit hole, then I do recommend my jazz chord books:

Guitar Chords in Context

Jazz Guitar Chord Mastery

And

Voice Leading Jazz Guitar.

All are published via **www.Fundamental-Changes.com** and available in paperback and Kindle editions.

Guitar Chords in Context is probably the next stage in your journey. It goes deeper into the theory and application of chords, and shows you how to construct and use pretty much every chord in modern guitar.

Jazz Guitar Chord Mastery introduces you to the concepts used by all jazz musicians when it comes to using voicings and inversions of the chords you know and love. If you want to add infinite colour to your palette and play all the inversions of Drop 2, Drop 3 and Drop 2+4 voicings on the guitar on every string group, this book is for you. It's extremely comprehensive and will change the way you look at the guitar neck forever.

Voice Leading Jazz Guitar is a bit different. It looks at how we can move between chords in the smoothest and most beautiful ways. You'll learn to view chords as movable structures and glide between them effortlessly by making instant substitutions and adding creative extensions. It's not for the faint-hearted, but it is how jazz giants like Ted Greene and Mike Walker view the guitar.

Practicing

My best advice is to use a metronome and a metronome only!

Unplug your guitar, set your metronome to about 60bpm and learn to hear the click as beats 2 and the 4 in the bar. You have to fill in the 1 and the 3 in your mind.

Count out loud and then start playing through your chosen progression. Don't stop if you make a mistake and keep the click on 2 and 4.

What this process teaches you is *independence*. You don't want to have to rely on the drummer to keep you in time, or the singer to let you know where you are in the tune.

With the metronome click, you're all on your own! It's tough at first, but once you get the hang of it, you'll improve *very* quickly.

Record yourself and listen back 24 hours later when you're less invested in your playing. It can be quite an eye opener!

There are some great apps out there for learning jazz. My favourite is iRealPro, available for Mac, PC and handheld devices. You can download all the chord charts you like and play along in any style. It's definitely worth checking out.

Above all, get in a band, even if it's just to jam at someone's house each week. You'll improve so much more quickly that way. Music is all about communication, and playing with a backing track in your bedroom can only teach you so much.

Have fun!

Joseph

Jazz Standards and Guitarists to Study

The following list of standards is a great starting point for your study of jazz guitar. Try to check out the original versions before going on to listen to different guitarists' interpretations of the pieces. These tunes represent a diverse range of musical approaches to jazz.

All The Things You Are	Just Friends
Alone Together	Misty
Autumn Leaves	My Funny Valentine
Billie's Bounce	Night and Day
Blue Bossa	Oleo
Body and Soul	On Green Dolphin Street
Bye Bye Blackbird	Recorda Me
Cherokee	Satin Doll
Confirmation	Scrapple From The Apple
Fly Me To The Moon	So What
Footprints	Solar
Four	St Thomas
Have You Met Miss Jones	Stella By Starlight
How High The Moon	The Girl From Ipanema
I'll Remember April	There Will Never Be Another You
If I Should Lose You	Up Jumped Spring
If I Were A Bell	Yesterdays

There are many influential jazz guitarists to check out, and the following list represents just the tip of the iceberg. Listen as much of their music as you can, and you'll get a comprehensive education in jazz guitar!

Wes Montgomery	Lenny Breau
Django Reinhardt	Kenny Burrell
Pat Metheny	Bill Frisell
Joe Pass	Larry Carlton
Charlie Christian	Pat Martino
John McLaughlin	Mike Stern
Allan Holdsworth	Larry Coryell
Grant Green	Tal Farlow
John Scofield	Freddie Green
Jim Hall	George Benson

Other Books from Fundamental Changes

The Complete Guide to Playing Blues Guitar Book One: Rhythm Guitar

The Complete Guide to Playing Blues Guitar Book Two: Melodic Phrasing

The Complete Guide to Playing Blues Guitar Book Three: Beyond Pentatonics

The Complete Guide to Playing Blues Guitar Compilation

The CAGED System and 100 Licks for Blues Guitar

Fundamental Changes in Jazz Guitar: The Major ii V I

Minor ii V Mastery for Jazz Guitar

Jazz Blues Soloing for Guitar

Guitar Scales in Context

Guitar Chords in Context

The First 100 Chords for Guitar

Jazz Guitar Chord Mastery

Complete Technique for Modern Guitar

Funk Guitar Mastery

The Complete Technique, Theory and Scales Compilation for Guitar

Sight Reading Mastery for Guitar

Rock Guitar Un-CAGED: The CAGED System and 100 Licks for Rock Guitar

The Practical Guide to Modern Music Theory for Guitarists

Beginner's Guitar Lessons: The Essential Guide

Chord Tone Soloing for Jazz Guitar

Heavy Metal Rhythm Guitar

Heavy Metal Lead Guitar

Progressive Metal Guitar

Heavy Metal Guitar Bible

Exotic Pentatonic Soloing for Guitar

Voice Leading Jazz Guitar

The Complete Jazz Soloing Compilation

The Jazz Guitar Chords Compilation

Fingerstyle Blues Guitar

The Complete DADGAD Guitar Method

Country Guitar for Beginners

Beginner Lead Guitar Method

The Chicago Blues Guitar Method

Beyond Rhythm Guitar

The Country Fingerstyle Guitar Method

Made in the USA
Columbia, SC
19 January 2024

30673336R00057